SHEDD AQUARIUM

KAREN FURNWEGER

BECKON BOOKS

Shedd
AQUARIUM

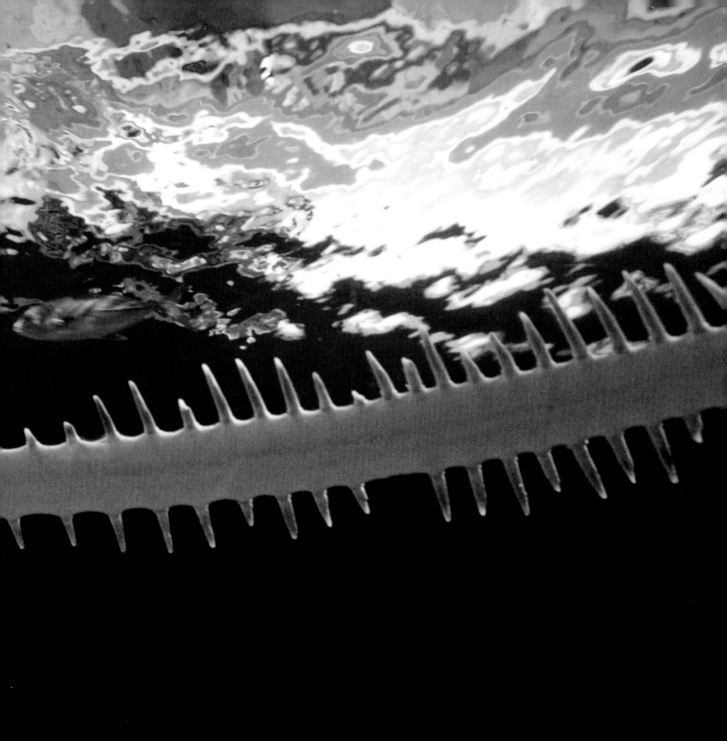

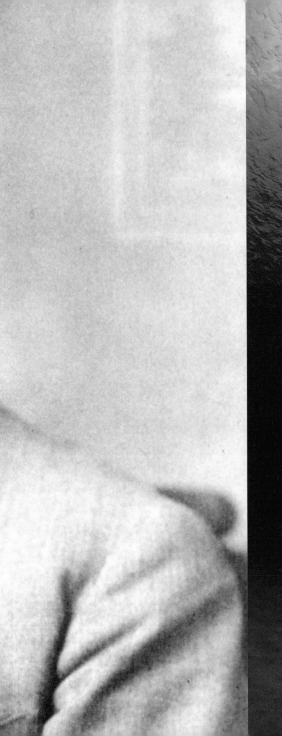

1
PART ONE

MR. SHEDD'S
GIFT

Far left: The aquarium's steel skeleton shows the beginnings of the octagonal dome and vaulted galleries.

Left: The elaborate bronze front doors are surrounded by *marble and topped with an intricate, realistic sculpted reef scene.*

Opposite: A busy day in the 1930s.

Shedd Aquarium's great bronze doors swung open to the public for the first time on December 19, 1929. Chicagoans had dug out from a blizzard just two days before, and they would be burdened for years to come by the stock market crash that had occurred two months earlier. A sneak preview of the new public aquarium—the world's largest—was a much-needed tonic. Only one exhibit, the tropical pool in the rotunda, was filled with animals. Yet people came in throngs throughout the holiday season to see the marble halls, skylight dome and bronze fixtures. This gorgeous building was theirs, and they embraced it.

Shedd officially opened on Memorial Day weekend 1930, and in the first six months, 2 million people flocked to see its fishes from far-off seas. As of 2010, more than 100 million people have enjoyed a day of aquatic adventures at Shedd. Still one of the world's largest indoor aquariums, it is home to more than 32,000 animals representing 1,500 species of fishes, invertebrates, amphibians, reptiles, birds, and marine and freshwater mammals. Shedd is a leader in the international zoo and aquarium community and is known for its award-winning exhibits, animal care and educational programs. It is even home to "Granddad," a fish still on exhibit that was acquired to wow the crowds at the World's Fair held in Chicago in 1933.

Now entering its ninth decade, Shedd Aquarium is a Chicago icon. Its great history began with an extraordinary gift to the city.

An Aquarium for Chicago

On January 24, 1924, John Graves Shedd, retired president of Marshall Field & Company, donated $2 million to build the world's largest aquarium for the people of Chicago. Shedd was among a group of civic-minded business leaders who strongly supported the young city's cultural growth. A self-made millionaire, he believed that "too many men have made fortunes in Chicago and while making them have left the city to grow as it would."

To ensure that his was a lasting gift to Chicago, he consulted with his peers. Together, they determined that every great city in the United States and Europe had a fine aquarium. Chicago must have the best. Shedd imagined a stately marble building and a collection of aquatic animals from around the world that would complement the two world-class institutions already in Grant Park—the Field Museum and the Art Institute of Chicago.

On February 11, 1924, the not-for-profit Shedd Aquarium Society was founded to construct, maintain and operate the aquarium. On the society's 15-member board was James Simpson, who had succeeded Shedd as president of Marshall Field's. Shedd gave Simpson the task of overseeing the construction of the aquarium. Simpson was a key figure in the city's progressive urban-planning movement and a skillful negotiator who paved the way for most of Chicago's public building projects in the 1920s and 1930s.

Even before Shedd's intentions were made public, Simpson got an enthusiastic, no-strings-attached go-ahead from Chicago mayor

William Hale "Big Bill" Thompson, a victory considering Thompson's administration was known more for its corruption than for its public works. Simpson then quickly arranged to have the South Park Commission, which later became part of a unified Chicago Park District, donate the circle of landfill it owned at the foot of 12th Street (now Roosevelt Road). He also hired the architectural firm of Graham, Anderson, Probst & White—the best in the Midwest at the time—to

> Shedd Aquarium has more than doubled in size, growing from 225,000 square feet when the original building was completed in 1929 to 480,500 square feet with the addition of the Oceanarium and Wild Reef.

design the building. Meanwhile, Shedd's new director, George F. Morse Jr., lobbied the Illinois General Assembly to approve legislation enabling the South Park Commission to levy a small tax—similar to funding given to Chicago's other museums—to maintain the new aquarium.

In September 1925 the Shedd Aquarium Society entered into contracts with John G. Shedd and the South Park Commission to build and stock a "high-grade aquarium," and Shedd wrote a check for $2 million. A year later, when rising costs threatened to scale back the size and quality of the building, Shedd readily supplied another $1 million, allowing construction to continue unchanged.

Lincoln Park Aquarium

In 1924 Chicago already had a new aquarium, which had been added to the Lincoln Park Zoo the year before. One of only seven public aquariums in the country at the time, and at 7,500 square feet the largest freshwater aquarium in the world, Lincoln Park drew about 2 million visitors a year. It featured an extensive collection of North American fishes as well as tropical fresh-water species. The basement of the handsome brick building also held a fish hatchery that produced 30 million fry, includ-ing salmon and several varieties of trout, whitefish and pike, for release into Lake Michigan and other northern Illinois waters each year.

The Lincoln Park Aquarium closed in 1936. Overshadowed by Shedd, it suffered from a lack of funds as the Great Depression dragged on. More-over, it had been ordered by the Chicago Board of Health to clean all the water it pumped from the lake by treating it with chlorine, which would have killed the fishes.

Left: The hatchery in the aquarium's basement was the main source of game fish for northern Illinois lakes and streams.

Below: On the main floor of Lincoln Park Aquarium, guests admire a trout exhibit, part of the finest trout collection in the United States in the 1920s and 1930s.

Opposite: The graceful brick building at Lincoln Park Zoo was the world's largest freshwater aquarium when it opened in 1923.

Shedd gratefully accepted Lincoln Park's entire collection of approximately 400 fishes. Shedd donated a matamata turtle when Chicago's original public aquarium reopened in 1937 as the Reptile House. Since 1998, the building has served as the zoo's café.

Right: The usually reserved John G. Shedd enjoys a lighthearted moment during an event at Wrigley Field.

The Merchant of Chicago

His name is chiseled in stone over the entrance to the aquarium. But who was John Graves Shedd? According to his boss, Marshall Field, Shedd was "the greatest merchant in the United States." As vice president of Marshall Field & Company, Shedd ran Chicago's famous department store. After Field died in 1906, Shedd succeeded him as president of the company, a post he held until he retired in 1923, when he became chairman of the board of directors.

Under Shedd's leadership, Marshall Field's grew from the largest store in Chicago to the largest wholesale and retail dry goods business in the world. In 1907 Shedd replaced the State Street store—built in the 1870s—with a luxurious modern building that boasted 35 acres of selling space. The national historic landmark, now occupied by Macy's, was designed by Ernest A. Graham, who would later design the aquarium as well as serve on its board.

Clearly, Shedd knew how to direct a successful business. Yet this great businessman came from humble beginnings. John G. Shedd was born in a frame farmhouse in Alstead, New Hampshire, on July 20, 1850. The youngest of eight children, he turned his back on farm work when he was 16 and set his sights on a business career. He worked at several dry goods stores in Vermont and New Hampshire, earning positions of increasing responsibility and saving most of his modest income. At night, he read textbooks to further his

education. By 1872, Shedd was ready for greater challenges and rewards than small-town New England could offer. In August of that year he headed west to Chicago to work for "the biggest store in town."

It was less than a year after the Great Fire of 1871 had leveled most of the city, and Chicago was rebuilding quickly. For an ambitious, imaginative young man, Chicago was a city of opportunity. Shedd walked into the Field, Leiter & Company store on State Street and asked Marshall Field for a job. As Shedd would later recount, Field asked the young man what he could do. "Sir, I can sell anything," he replied with confidence. Field hired him as a

$10-dollar-a-week salesman and stock boy with a note to his supervisor to raise his weekly salary in six months "if suits" or "let him go at any time if does not suit."

Shedd, whose rural New England background and earnest work ethic mirrored Field's, "suited" very well: Field raised his pay three times in the first year. Within the store's large wholesale operation, Shedd advanced to head of the important laces and linens department and then to general manager of the entire wholesale business. In 1893 he was made a partner in the company, and in 1901 he became vice president under Field himself.

Shedd had a strong sense of civic responsibility. He began the store's tradition of public service to the community. For his employees, he established a branch of the Chicago Public Library at the store, along with a gymnasium and a junior academy that allowed young workers to earn the equivalent

> In 1985 John G. Shedd was elected posthumously to the National Freshwater Fishing Hall of Fame in the category of Organization and Education. The Wisconsin organization cited Shedd's generous funding of a "world-class aquarium committed to education about the aquatic environment."

of a high school diploma. Because he had had no source of good books as a boy, he donated a library to his hometown of Alstead. And he gave generously to his adopted city, donating tens of thousands of dollars to the University of Chicago, the Art Institute of Chicago and the YMCA.

Shedd was a member of the Commercial Club of Chicago, which commissioned Daniel Burnham's visionary 1909 Plan for Chicago—the now-famous Burnham Plan—and was appointed to the Chicago Plan Commission to put it into effect. Charles H. Wacker, chairman of the commission, said, "Mr. Shedd's interest in the Chicago Plan never flagged. He took great satisfaction out of the plan improvements, as they were realized one by one, for no one understood better than he their significance in the life and growth of the city he loved."

The centerpiece of the Chicago Plan was the lakefront, and here Shedd made his greatest contribution: the aquarium. Yet he never saw more

> John G. Shedd's widow, Mary R. Shedd, gave generously to the aquarium, especially during the lean years of the Great Depression. Shedd's daughters, Helen Shedd Reed (later Helen Shedd Keith) and Laura Shedd Schweppe, contributed $400,000 early in 1930 to help purchase the animal collection. Mrs. Keith also provided for the Aquatic Education Center, which opened in 1975.

than the architects' first drawings. Shedd died of complications from appendicitis on October 22, 1926. Just 10 days earlier, as he left his office at Marshall Field's, he had expressed his desire to see the aquarium completed.

His death was front-page news, and on the day of his funeral, store employees were given the day off to honor the slight, white-haired man who had told them, "I would like you to remember that this store is only what the people of Chicago, the West, and the nation have made it. It was founded to render a public service."

John G. Shedd was buried at Rosehill Cemetery on Chicago's North Side. Thirteen months later, ground was broken for his aquarium.

2
PART TWO

CHICAGO'S INLAND SEA

Far left: In early 1926 Shedd's associate director, Walter H. Chute (center), and Mario J. Schiavoni (left), project designer for architects Graham, Anderson, Probst & White, set off on a tour of West Coast aquariums. Pictured with them is Shedd's first director, George F. Morse.

Left: The original tropical pool in the rotunda was based on similar features in European aquariums.

Opposite: A page from Chute's small leather trip notebook contains sketches of the then-new Steinhart Aquarium in San Francisco.

Creating the world's largest—and finest—aquarium more than a

thousand miles from any seacoast required three years of research and careful planning. After forming the Shedd Aquarium Society in 1924, John G. Shedd and the society's directors hired George F. Morse Jr., former director of the Boston Zoological Park, the South Boston Aquarium and the brand-new Brookfield Zoo, to be the director of the new aquarium. The next year, Morse recruited Walter H. Chute, his successor at the Boston Aquarium. Shedd and James Simpson were impressed with Chute and appointed him associate director.

More than anyone else, Chute influenced how the aquarium looks and operates today. Traveling with an engineer from Graham, Anderson, Probst & White, he toured the leading aquariums in Europe to study their design, construction and management during October and November of 1925. The men also visited the aquariums in New York, Boston, Philadelphia, Detroit and San Francisco. Chute made detailed notes and sketches in a small loose-leaf notebook.

Back in Chicago, he worked side by side with the architects to incorporate the best of the classic designs with state-of-the-art water filtration systems, spacious work areas for the animal care staff and wide viewing spaces for aquarium guests. Shedd and the society board approved the first sketches for the aquarium in the fall of 1926, just weeks before Shedd's death. Plans were completed in July 1927, and construction began on November 2, 1927. In 1928 Morse resigned, and Chute was made director, a post he held for 36 years.

San Francisco Aquarium.

Situated in beautiful Golden Gate Park.
Built by private bequest. Maintainance by
City - controlled by Cal. Academy of Science.
Central building of a group of three, two of
which are completed. Court yard in center of group
with three out door pools for seals and sea-lions.

Entrance opens into a very attractive tropical
swamp. Three entrances lead from swamp
room to main exhibition hall. No provision
made to control crowds. Difference of opinion
among the staff as to the efficiency of this
arrangement.

Floor of entrance and main hall set with
soft tile with an occasional figure of crab, sea horse
etc. Shows serious signs of wearing although

The building was completed in two years. But the projected October 1, 1929, opening date came and went due to delays in getting tank materials, life-support equipment—and salt water, which had to be shipped in railroad cars from Key West, Florida. When the first five-car shipment arrived on December 10, Shedd Aquarium Society president Melvin A. Traylor announced that the rotunda would be open to the public on December 19. "The public must understand, however," Traylor cautioned, "that the exhibition tanks proper are not yet ready and that for the present, the display of marine life will be very limited."

In fact, the only display was a 40-foot-diameter freshwater pool in the rotunda, featuring native fishes, reptiles and amphibians among tropical plants. Even after the vast reservoirs were filled with seawater and the water-circulation systems were running, the new concrete tanks had to stabilize chemically before any marine fishes could be brought in.

Collecting finally began in the spring of 1930, the first of what would become two major collecting trips a year. On May 30, 1930, the first of the six galleries officially opened in a ceremony attended by Shedd's widow, Mary R. Shedd, and other family members. The final two galleries opened five months later—after 160 carloads of salt water had been delivered—in October 1930.

The balanced aquarium room, featuring small freshwater exhibits similar to home aquariums (later renamed Tributaries), opened on June 1, 1931. With it, John G. Shedd's intentions were fully realized. Shedd Aquarium not only housed the greatest variety of sea life under one roof—at the time exhibiting 5,000 animals, representing 400 to 450 species—but it was also the first inland aquarium to maintain a permanent exhibit of marine and freshwater fishes, from both the Atlantic and Pacific Oceans. It was also the first to devote an entire room to the display of balanced aquariums.

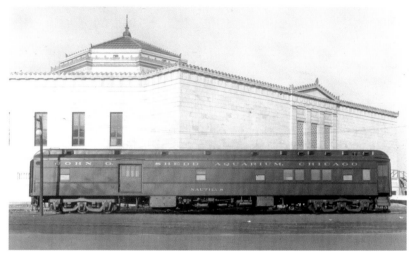

Gathering the Collection

Shedd Aquarium collecting trips are a tradition that dates from the earliest days of the institution. At first, collecting was a necessity: Many exotic species were not available through wholesalers or by trading with other aquariums. Today collecting continues to be an important method for Shedd to obtain its unique display of aquatic life from around the world.

Traveling with Nautilus

Most of the first marine fishes on exhibit arrived on the *Nautilus*, a Pullman train car custom-built for long-range collecting trips. Before the days of air freight, Shedd could not have maintained its saltwater collection without this railroad car. From its maiden trip to Key West in April 1930 until it was retired in 1957, the *Nautilus* traveled approximately 20,000 miles a year to Maine, Florida and California as well as around the Midwest. Built by Pullman Car Works in Chicago for about $30,000, the *Nautilus* was fitted with tanks, pumps, air compressors, electric refrigeration coils and steam heat for an additional $10,000. It could accommodate cold and tropical saltwater fishes and cold, temperate and tropical freshwater species. During the aquarium's first four years, the *Nautilus* transported more than 21,000 fishes, mostly tropical marine species. Walter H. Chute called it "a miniature traveling aquarium."

Two-thirds of the 83-foot car was allocated to life-support equipment and tanks—sixteen 200-gallon waterproof cypress boxes that rolled on and off the car and a score of 30-gallon metal containers.

Far left: An 1873 engraving depicts an unlikely display of marine life—on wheels!

Left: The interior of Detroit's Belle Isle Aquarium, built in 1904, influenced the design of Shedd. The Michigan aquarium closed in 2005.

The Dawning of the Age of Aquariums

The Victorians of the mid-19th century were fascinated with the natural world that global exploration was opening up to them. Zoos were wildly popular, and once people understood how to care for aquatic animals, large-scale exhibits of never-before-seen marine life became the rage.

The term "aquarium" first appeared in the writings of Philip Gosse, a 19th-century English naturalist. Gosse helped establish the first public aquarium at the London Zoological Society in 1853. At first, the aquarium building boom was limited to coastal cities with ready access to seawater. Gosse solved that problem by adding a combination of sea salts to clean fresh water, a procedure still used by inland aquariums today. England's Brighton Aquarium, the largest in the world when it opened in 1872, displayed dolphins, sharks, sea turtles and scores of fishes.

By the early 1900s, there were aquariums from Paris to Tokyo. In 1856 P. T. Barnum

Left: A 1930s poster promotes the Fairmount Park Aquarium in Philadelphia.

Far left: Located on England's southeast coast, the Brighton Aquarium (with clock tower) was an instant success when it opened in 1872. There, fishes and marine mammals were displayed in extravagant Victorian exhibit halls. It has been replaced by the modern Brighton Sea Life Centre.

opened the first aquarium in the United States in New York City. In 1873 the nation's first public aquarium, National Aquarium in Washington, D.C., opened in Woods Hole, Massachusetts. It was moved to the Washington Mall in 1888 and has been housed in the U.S. Department of Commerce building since 1932.

Soon aquariums sprang up around the country: New York Aquarium (1896); Waikiki Aquarium in the territory of Hawaii and Belle Isle Aquarium in Detroit (1904); Point Defiance Zoo and Aquarium in Tacoma, Washington (1905); Memphis Zoological Garden and Aquarium (1906); South Boston Aquarium (1912); Steinhart Aquarium in San Francisco and Chicago's Lincoln Park Aquarium (1923); Columbus Zoo's aquarium (1927); Shedd Aquarium (1930); and Dallas Aquarium (1936). It took the global economic crisis of the 1930s, followed by World War II, to bring the great wave of aquarium building to an end.

The remainder of the car was outfitted to serve as simple living quarters for the six-person collecting crew, with bunks, a bath and a kitchenette. Fully loaded, the *Nautilus* carried 4,500 gallons of water. But the seawater that sloshed during the April-to-November collecting seasons, along with exposure to the elements during winters spent in the Illinois Central Railroad yard, eventually took a toll. In 1957, rusted beyond repair, the car was taken out of service.

With the staff unable to make long-distance collecting trips and some of the saltwater exhibits sitting empty, the aquarium's board of trustees searched for an affordable replacement. They found it in a retired stainless-steel lunch car, which they purchased and had refitted by the Thrall Car Manufacturing Company for $175,000. Hitched to a high-speed passenger train, the *Nautilus II* made its first run to Florida in May 1959 for a collecting trip to Bimini in the Bahamas. That car reached the end of its line in 1972, the victim of deterioration and discontinued rail routes. In 1975 the *Nautilus II* was donated to the Monticello Railway Museum near Champaign, Illinois, where it is on exhibit and open to the public.

Two Shedd grandsons, John Shedd Schweppe and John Shedd Reed, served on the aquarium's board of trustees, the latter as president of the board from 1984 to 1994, overseeing the Oceanarium project.

Coral Reef Collections

By the time the second railroad car was retired, two significant factors were changing the way the aquarium collected animals. First, air freight was becoming a cheaper, faster alternative to rail transport.

Filling the Inland Sea

In early 1930, a million gallons of ocean water were moved 1,600 miles by rail from the Florida Keys to Grant Park and pumped into Shedd's massive reservoirs. Although synthetic salt water was available, aquarium officials had chosen natural seawater, which guaranteed the proper salinity. To complete the task, the aquarium borrowed 20 railroad tank cars from the Union Tank Car Company. The insulated cars maintained the 75-degree water temperature to keep the natural microscopic marine life in the water alive. The shipment cost about $50,000, or four cents a gallon.

Over the years, both natural seawater and a synthetic mix— the latter a combination of Lake Michigan water and 11 sea salts formulated by Walter H. Chute—replaced day-to-day water losses. In November 1970 a barge carrying 800,000 gallons of seawater from the Gulf of Mexico arrived at Monroe Harbor. The Chicago Fire

Shedd Aquarium Formula — Artificial Sea Water

106.8 gal. S.G.=1.026 166.6...

Absolute salt percentage required?	Use:	Grams.	Absolute Salts obtained Total Grams.	Ultimate Analysis % of Residue
NaCl- 77.70	"K.D. Anchor" Brand Granular Salt. (99.67% NaCl.) — Morton Salt Co.	10,905.	10,869.	Na 30.484
MgCl₂-10.85	Magnesium Chloride, Pure Crystals. M.C.W. (46.81% MgCl₂)	3,241.	1,517.1	Mg 3.733
MgSO₄- 4.70	Magnesium Sulphate, U.S.P.XI Granul. M.C.W. (48.82% mgso)	1,323.	645.9	Ca 1.291
CaSO₄-3.70	Calcium Sulphate, Pure Precip. 2H₂O. M.C.W. (79.05% CaSO₄)	654.	517.0	K 1.110
K₂SO₄-2.47	Potassium Sulphate, N.F.VI Powder. M.C.W. (99.52% K₂SO₄)	346.	344.3	Cl 54.955
NaBr-0.25	Sodium Bromide, U.S.P.XI Granular. (99.5% NaBr)	35.	34.8	SO₄ 7.850
CaCO₃-0.31	Calcium Carbonate, Precip. U.S.P.XI. Used in excess	45.	52.0	CO₃ 0.370
NaF-.002	Sodium Fluoride, Pure powder. (as 100%)	0.3	0.3	Br 0.192
PO₄-.014	Phosphoric Acid, 85% U.S.P.XI	2.0	1.7	F 0.001
KIO₃.004	Potassium Iodate, pure M.C.W. (as 100%)	0.6	0.6	I 0.0025
Na₂CO₃-qs	Sufficient to adjust pH value.			PO₄ 0.012
Total-100%	Incidental constituents in above salts — Salts in 100 gallons Lake Water other than CO₃.		33.0	Total 100.000%
	Fluorine = 0.35 p.p.m.		41.6	
	Iodine = 0.916 p.p.m. (SEE OTHER SIDE) — Total Absolute Salts		14,057.3	
	Salinity = 3.62% at 100 gal.			

Procedure: Dissolve all of the Salts, in a large portion of the water, except the Calcium Carbonate, which will only partially dissolve. Mix thoroly and add Lake water to make up 100 gallons exactly. Allow chalk to settle and decant or syphon off the cleared product. Adjust pH value if necessary.

The formula on this sheet was very carefully calculated and makes allowance for salts in the Lake water as well as incidental salts in the commercial products specified to be used. The ultimate analysis is accurately computed, arrived at merely by calculations, and conform to typical sea water analyses.

The idea has been advanced (see Wieand and Whipple, F.W. Biology, page 38) that certain carbohydrates are present in natural waters and may play an important role in the respiration processes of animals. Experiments seem to bear this out. It is common knowledge that something is missing in artificial sea water, which has a decided biological importance. Hence, no harm can be done and possibly great benefit derived by adding to this formula a small quantity of cane sugar, say 0.3 or 0.4 gm.

The following elements are present in natural sea water and some of them may have biological importance but they are presently in the Lake water and salts used in sufficient quantities.
Iron, Copper, Silver, manganese, Silicon, Zinc, aluminum, Barium, Strontium, Lithium, Boron and Cæsium.

Rubidium is present in sea water, perhaps as much as 0.004% of the residue. However, it is of doubtful value biologically, at least, no references to it are available and its cost is prohibitive.

Calculation for 100 gallon formula:
100 gals fresh lake water weighs - 378,543 grams.
378,543 X 1.0265 (S.G.) = 388,580.
Hence 100 gals of normal sea water wgs - 388,580 gms.
If the salinity is selected - 3.62% then
388,580 X .0362 = 14,067 gms = residue or total absolute salts required.
Other quantities than 100 gals. may be easily calculated as the unit of weight is the convenient grams.

Department provided 1,000 feet of hose to pump the water into the building. It was the last time Shedd used ocean water. Synthetic seawater finally became more cost-effective.

Making it, however, was labor-intensive. Several times a year, aquarists mixed a 110,000-gallon batch of salt water, a task that took up to three weeks and involved dissolving 13 tons of sodium chloride, along with 20 other mineral ingredients, into a reservoir of lake water.

Today Shedd uses a commercial sea salt mix. When the aquarium's engineers refilled the Oceanarium's pools after the building's 2009 renovation, they dissolved nearly 500 tons of "instant seawater" mix into 3.2 million gallons of fresh water. The resulting 3.5 percent salinity replicates ocean water as closely as possible.

Left: Shedd's custom-designed research vessel, the R/V Coral Reef II, is a floating field camp and temporary aquarium capable of holding hundreds of marine animals. Based in Miami, the boat has a cruising radius of 2,000 miles.

Opposite, far right and right: One-ton beluga Naluark and his trainer are lifted from a water-filled blue transport container—called a "cradle"—as the whale returns to Shedd from Mystic Aquarium. Inside Shedd, a built-in crane carries Naluark to a pool where he's welcomed home by trainers.

And second, many of Shedd's tried-and-true collecting spots in the Bahamas were turning into resorts. The arrival of masses of boaters, divers and sport fishermen, as well as rapid coastal development and habitat decline, had chased away many species, making it necessary for the aquarium's collectors to travel farther and spend more time—and money—to find them.

In 1970 director William P. Braker asked the board of trustees for a collecting vessel. A 7-year-old private yacht, the *Mohini*, was purchased, rechristened the R/V *Coral Reef* and refitted for collecting expeditions. The boat gave aquarists enormous mobility, allowing them to collect a wider variety of fishes and invertebrates. In addition, both the people and the animals benefited from the amenities of a real collecting boat—large holding tanks with life-support systems, facilities for trawling and diving, and decent living quarters. The R/V *Coral Reef* was in service for

When it opened in 1930, Shedd's state-of-the-art aquatic life-support equipment included "mechanical refrigeration." Designed by William H. Carrier, a noted air-conditioning engineer from Newark, New Jersey, the refrigeration installation kept the various saltwater and freshwater systems at consistently the right temperatures.

about a decade. Mounting maintenance problems, including damage done by shipworms to its wooden hull, led to the yacht's sale in 1982.

The next year, the board of trustees approved the construction of a new collecting and research vessel, the R/V *Coral Reef II*. The 80-foot blue-and-white aluminum-hulled boat was launched in September 1984. It features an 1,800-gallon specimen tank in the main deck, five 150-gallon live wells flanking the deckhouse and a filtered life-support system that can operate on open seawater or as a recirculating closed system. Its cabins can accommodate 11 passengers and three crew members. The boat has a dive platform, onboard air compressors, scuba tanks, and trawls, seines and other collecting gear. It also carries two small motorized boats for expeditions into shallow waters. In addition to being available for

Shedd's collecting, research and education trips, the R/V *Coral Reef II* is chartered by other aquariums, colleges and research institutions.

When Whales Fly

Starting with the transport of its first two beluga whales from Churchill, Manitoba, in 1989, Shedd has refined and defined the process of moving marine mammals by air.

Several of Shedd's belugas have flown to aquariums on either coast as participants in a cooperative breeding program among six North American aquariums and zoos. But it was the total renovation of the Oceanarium that necessitated the most ambitious and tightly choreographed transport in the 20 years of Shedd's marine mammals program.

The aquarium had to move seven beluga whales, four Pacific white-sided dolphins, five sea otters—and their 16 trainers. Twice. The belugas and dolphins were moved to temporary quarters at Connecticut's Mystic Aquarium during two separate flights, while the sea otters traveled 416 miles by refrigerated truck to the Minnesota Zoo.

The otters are trained to romp in and out of transport kennels for regular medical exams, and they had plenty of cracked ice to play with on the trip. So for them, the eight-hour drive was a nonevent. Moving the whales and dolphins was more challenging. Three of the belugas—those born at Shedd—had never flown, and two were calves that were still nursing.

Six months before the move, all three whales were enrolled in "flight school." They practiced moving in and out of custom-fitted padded stretchers and spending increasing lengths of time in them while trainers simulated the kinds of activity the whales would experience during the real move. The preparation paid off: During the flight to Mystic, the whales were as relaxed as seasoned travelers.

Not long after the animals were settled into their temporary pools, planning began for the return trips. The long punch list included scheduling cargo jets and ground crews; lining up 40,000-pound forklifts to move the animals' water-filled transport "cradles"—weighing up to 6 tons each—on and off planes; and arranging for police-escorted truck convoys to carry animals and staff members to and from airports.

Each homecoming transport took about 24 hours from the time the flatbed trucks carrying the transport cradles were positioned alongside the animals' pools at Mystic until the last beluga whale slipped into the water at Shedd. Throughout the 1,000-mile trip, a trainer rode with each animal in its cradle.

Shedd's green araçari, opposite, an internationally protected species, was acquired from a private aviculturist. The fruit-eating bird's favorite foods are also those that can contain the highest levels of pesticides, so he eats an all-organic diet.

A Sustainable Collection

In addition to its annual collecting trip in the Bahamas, Shedd acquires its animals from many other sources: breeding programs, sister aquariums, wholesale dealers, professional breeders, and state and federal wildlife agencies. Shedd's acquisition policy is based on best sustainable practices.

Many once-abundant aquatic species are in serious decline due to the degradation of marine and freshwater habitats, unsustainable commercial fishing and irresponsible collecting practices for the pet trade. Other threats to animal populations in the wild include the emerging impact of climate change.

Breeding programs, both in-house and in collaboration with other aquariums, are the most

sustainable sources of animals. Shedd's many breeding programs include corals, freshwater rays, caiman lizards and beluga whales. Thanks to its record-setting success with zebra sharks, 16 other aquariums in the United States have housed Shedd offspring rather than collecting these fish from the wild.

Of course, aquariums do not have the knowledge or the resources to breed all the animals they exhibit. Sometimes Shedd turns to professional breeders for tropical fishes, amphibians, reptiles and birds. Government fish hatcheries contribute to Shedd's local freshwater fishes collection. Many other species still can be sustainably collected in the wild, and Shedd works with licensed collectors and wholesalers who can document that the animals were collected legally from healthy populations, using methods that did not harm other wildlife or habitats.

The opposite of sustainability is wildlife smuggling, a multibillion-dollar business. When illegally imported sea turtles, fishes and corals are intercepted and confiscated by the U.S. Fish and Wildlife Service at O'Hare International Airport, their next stop is Shedd Aquarium. Shedd's aquarists help federal wildlife agents identify rare species, which helps to prosecute and convict smugglers. They also provide accommodations for the animals in legal limbo. USFWS donates seized animals to Shedd and other aquariums for display.

Through its sustainable collection practices, Shedd sets an example of responsible stewardship, both for the species in its exhibits and their counterparts in the wild.

3
PART THREE

NEPTUNE'S
TEMPLE

Far left and left: The aquarium's architects decorated every surface and fixture with images of aquatic life, including a petite seahorse on a bronze entry lantern and a golden dolphin on a red-tiled façade in the old Tributaries room.

Opposite: The rotunda, shown with its 80-foot-wide skylight, was restored to its original glory in 1999. Shedd's Caribbean Reef exhibit received a state-of-the-art renovation at the same time.

Shedd Aquarium was designed by the Chicago-based architectural firm of Graham, Anderson, Probst & White. The firm's other local work includes the Field Museum, the Wrigley Building, the Museum of Science and Industry and the Merchandise Mart. Many of Graham, Anderson, Probst & White's buildings, including the aquarium, have been designated national historic landmarks by the National Park Service.

An example of the Greek- and Roman-inspired Beaux Arts architecture that was promoted by Chicago architect Daniel Burnham at the turn of the 20th century, Shedd Aquarium is perhaps the firm's grandest effort. Ernest Graham, one of Burnham's former assistants, stayed faithful to the style while making adjustments to reflect the nature of the building. The front of the aquarium features elements of a classic Greek temple, including Doric columns that support the entrance portico. The broad staircase leading to the entrance reflects the ancient Greek practice of placing temples on platforms to distinguish them as important buildings.

The aquarium's layout follows a traditional Greek floor plan: Designed as a circle in a cross, the centerpiece of the building is a great foyer with three pairs of galleries extending from a rotunda. From there, the architects created an octagon, filling in the corners of the cross to create work areas for the staff, including food-storage and preparation rooms and a fish hospital. The 80-foot-wide glass dome that crowns the 100-foot-high rotunda repeats the octagon.

At every turn, the architects incorporated aquatic touches into the traditional design. Waves roll up the outside of the dome to Neptune's trident. Sea turtles, fishes and sea stars appear in the bronze doors, ceiling panels, chandeliers and terra cotta trim. Chicago was a leading supplier of terra cotta, and some of the country's finest artists produced the white-glazed clay animals, shells and other ornamentation that adorn the building. Walter H. Chute, aquarium director from 1928 until 1964, oversaw construction and worked closely with local sculptor Eugene Romero to make sure the sea creatures portrayed in terra cotta, plaster and bronze were true to life.

The rotunda originally housed a 40-foot-diameter sunken tropical pool, called the "swamp scene" in-house, that was filled with tropical plants, freshwater fishes, frogs and turtles, and was flooded with natural light from the glass dome. In 1971 the pool was replaced with the 90,000-gallon Caribbean Reef, one of the country's first large multispecies exhibits. To highlight the artificially illuminated reef exhibit—and slow algae growth—the inside of the dome was blacked out and the walls above the marble wainscoting were painted dark green. Once the brightest and most elegant space

in the aquarium, the rotunda was hidden in darkness. In 1999, while the Caribbean Reef underwent a renovation, the rotunda and dome were restored to their opening-day glory, with new lighting that can either highlight the architecture or be dimmed during dive presentations in the Caribbean Reef.

With their brightly lighted exhibit windows, Shedd's original long, darkened galleries are typical of the traditional European aquariums. Art museums also influenced the design of the galleries, encouraging guests to move from one framed window of beautiful sea creatures to the next, as if they were looking at paintings. Educational graphics were limited to a picture of each animal and its name in English and Latin.

Years later, two developments in the way animals are exhibited would change the shape of aquariums: a new type of aquatic display facility that featured marine mammals, and the immersive exhibit, which permitted visitors to walk through rather than in front of a natural-looking animal display.

The Oceanarium

Director William P. Braker had a vision: whales and dolphins on view along Chicago's lakefront. In 1986, with the approval and support of the staff, the board of trustees, city, state and federal governments, and the Chicago philanthropic community, a magnificent marine mammal pavilion took shape in blueprints and three-dimensional models.

The architectural firm of Lohan Associates faced several design challenges in constructing the Oceanarium: The addition needed to satisfy the spatial, physiological and psychological needs of a variety of cold-ocean mammals and birds; it had to complement, not compete with, a national historic landmark; and finally, it had to occupy land that at the time did not exist.

The rotunda's illuminated clock and bronze skate sconces that hold nautilus-shaped shades of capiz shell, opposite, recall the work of Louis Comfort Tiffany. While the aquarium's exquisite bronze fixtures are not authentic Tiffany pieces, they are masterful imitations created by the Superb Bronze & Iron Company.

The only way to expand was into the lake, enlarging the circle of landfill on which the aquarium sits. On September 17, 1987, 60 years after the groundbreaking for the aquarium, the underwater cornerstone for the Oceanarium's seawall was dropped into Lake Michigan. The area for the new building was enclosed with sheets of steel that were driven into the lake's clay bottom. Thirty million gallons of water were pumped out of the newly created "Lake Shedd," and 22,000 cubic yards of landfill were dumped in.

To leave the front view of the landmark unchanged, the Oceanarium was designed to fan out from the back wall of the aquarium. The roofline of the four-story addition was kept lower than the original building to allow a graceful and respectful transition from old to new, and the classical and contemporary styles were linked architecturally by finishing the Oceanarium's exterior with the white Georgia marble stripped from the construction side of the aquarium. The original thick slabs were sliced into

thinner sections, providing just enough marble to cover the north and south sides of the new building.

Whereas the original aquarium building was designed as an elegant setting for nearly 200 exhibit tanks, the Oceanarium's interior is one sweeping exhibit. Guests can peer into large pools as they stroll along "nature trails" that curve through a re-created Pacific Northwest coastal ecosystem. The 2-million-gallon Whale Harbor appears to flow directly into Lake Michigan. Thanks to 160-foot roof trusses that eliminate the need for support columns, guests in the Oceanarium's amphitheater can easily view the aquatic animal shows from any seat.

Polar Play Zone, a permanent children's exhibit that opened in 2009, fills the lower level with a touch pool, hands-on exhibits and play areas alongside the penguin habitat. It also features underwater viewing windows to the beluga, dolphin and sea otter pools.

> The original aquarium building cost $3 million to build in the late 1920s. Fifty years later, it was estimated that the price tag would be more than $24 million. Today, at approximately $750 a square foot, it would cost at least $225 million to duplicate the 300-foot-diameter octagonal building of white Georgia marble.

With its well-planned architecture and unobstructed views, the Oceanarium is a wonderful complement to the original building. This addition changed the character as well as the shape of Shedd Aquarium, putting it again at the forefront of the world's state-of-the-art animal exhibits. Annual attendance shot from an average of 925,000 in the 1970s and 1980s to 2 million since the 1991 opening. But while the Oceanarium raised the bar for new major exhibits at Shedd, it also raised the question of how—and where—to create more immersive exhibits.

Amazon Rising: Seasons of the River

Soon after becoming president and CEO in 1994, Ted A. Beattie, with the board of trustees, spearheaded a master plan to take Shedd into the 21st century. It evaluated the strengths of Shedd's existing collection, its husbandry expertise, the opportunities to display new species at Shedd and the

public interest. In doing so, the plan identified two ecosystems—the Amazon River and Philippines coral reefs—for new major exhibits.

After an extensive study involving architects, structural engineers, trustees, an architectural historian and aquarium guests, Beattie gave the go-ahead early in 1999 to gut the original Galleries 1 and 2 to create Amazon Rising. The walk-through exhibit, which depicts a year in an Amazon floodplain forest from low-water season through the floods, opened in spring of 2000.

Year-round, the exhibit's 75-degree temperature and 50 percent humidity envelope guests in a steamy Amazon environment tailored to the needs of 250 species of animals. With its floor-to-ceiling exhibits, where piranhas, stingrays and river turtles swim above eye level, it is hard to believe that Amazon Rising is under the familiar canopy of the Shedd galleries.

The exhibit does retain its historical look: The barrel-vaulted ceilings are still there. But behind-the-scenes work areas were opened up to create sunny new exhibit space under the original skylights.

With Amazon Rising, Shedd entered a new realm of exhibition. The Amazon's annual floods support the greatest diversity of freshwater animals in the world. To represent the interconnectedness of aquatic, terrestrial and arboreal species within this fluctuating ecosystem, Shedd exhibited tropical birds and primates alongside fishes, amphibians and reptiles for the first time. In addition, throughout the exhibit, evidence of the local ribereños, most notably an authentic stilt-leg house from the Peruvian Amazon, emphasizes that people are an integrated part of the environment.

Wild Reef: Sharks at Shedd and Corals, Too

For the second expansion in its history, Shedd went underground. Wild Reef was built 25 feet below street level under a slightly extended south terrace. Like the Oceanarium, Wild Reef is not visible from the front of the building, an effort to preserve Shedd's landmark

appearance. The compact two-level structure sits on a 13,500-square-foot footprint. The lower exhibit level has eight main habitat areas containing 575,000 gallons of salt water, while the tops of the habitats open to the upper-level life-support and work areas, giving aquarists easy access to the animals.

The public area was designed to make guests feel as if they are diving the coral reefs of the Philippines—the most diverse ecosystem on Earth. Colorful re-creations of 85 coral species encrust the walls and ceilings, blurring the line between inside and outside the habitats. In addition to the meticulously crafted artificial corals, Wild Reef is home to 60 species of live corals. These have created a colorful reef that pulses to the gentle current in the 6,000-gallon habitat.

Corals have built-in gardens in the form of algae in their cells. These algae use tropical sunshine to photosynthesize food that is used by the corals. At Shedd, the corals thrive in the intense light of a dozen metal halide bulbs, totaling 8,400 watts.

In the central 400,000-gallon seafloor habitat, only 5½ inches of acrylic separate Shedd's guests from Wild Reef's 20 sharks and other large predators. Under the 12-foot arching windows, guests can see huge rays overhead—the 8-foot white-spotted guitarfish and the 13-foot endangered green sawfish. Steps away, smaller blue-spotted rays swim underfoot in a sunken, glass-covered pool in this vivid depiction of Neptune's kingdom.

The Oceanarium Reimagined

The Oceanarium renovation started out as an ambitious enough project to "scrub the tub"—or, temporarily relocate 150 animals, drain 3 million gallons of salt water and redo the 17-year-old coating on all the pools.

A Green Museum

Sustainability is integrated into every aspect of Shedd's operations. A comprehensive energy-reduction plan has cut total energy consumption by 79 percent since 1996. Innovative changes include turning off the mechanical water chillers when the outside temperature drops below 40 degrees and routing exhibit water to a rooftop cooling tower. That's at least five months of free chilled water for the belugas, penguins, octopuses and other cold-ocean animals.

Shedd became the first public building in Chicago to install a nontoxic, nonpolluting polymer roof made from soybeans. Unlike petroleum-based black asphalt roofs, which get so hot in the summer

Right: Prickly pear cacti are among the drought-resistant native plants in a dune garden that recalls a Great Lakes shore ecosystem.

that they actually raise the city's air temperature, this tofu-colored roof reflects sunlight, reducing the aquarium's need for air-conditioning.

The new office suite built atop the Oceanarium is being considered for the U.S. Green Buildings Council's coveted Leadership in Energy and Environmental Design (LEED) certification. Upgrades to the original aquarium building, from using low-VOC paint to retrofitting washrooms with low-volume fixtures, meet LEED standards for existing buildings.

Outside the building, Shedd shows guests how to have a greener garden using less water and no chemicals through its award-winning landscapes. Native plants attract butterflies, birds and other wildlife, while a rain garden collects storm water runoff from the aquarium's terrace—and keeps it out of Lake Michigan.

Shedd has been certified as a "Green Museum" by the City of Chicago for its commitment to environmentally sustainable business practices.

Right: In the company of a trainer, guests can meet, touch and feed one of Shedd's whales in a private habitat during the popular beluga encounter program.

Soon, however, it blossomed into an opportunity to update, upgrade and completely reimagine Shedd's most popular exhibit from top to bottom.

Shedd's nine-month, $50 million renovation transformed the Oceanarium's space and spirit. It added roaring sea lions; new penguins; state-of-the-art theatrical technology for aquatic animal shows; redesigned dining facilities with an attached lakefront terrace; a permanent children's exhibit; a private pool for guests to have an in-water encounter with a beluga whale; and a

Reimagining the Oceanarium included creating a multimedia aquatic show highlighting the dolphins, beluga whales, penguins and other guest favorites. High-tech lighting, video projection and audio equipment, and possibly the world's longest Roman curtain across the 475-foot glass wall, transform the amphitheater into a magical setting.

waterfall ending in a 2,500-gallon estuary habitat with a new display of Pacific Northwest fishes and invertebrates. Behind the scenes, new life-support systems for the animals were installed.

Even though the renovation kept the Oceanarium closed for the first five months of 2009, attendance for the year hit 1.96 million, exceeding Shedd's expectations and maintaining its position as the number 1 cultural attraction in Chicago. Both local and out-of-town guests poured in—including a record-setting 25,930 one Friday—to see the reopened exhibit.

Left: Inside Polar Play Zone's 15-foot submarine, Shedd Explorer, *kids find lots of hands-on activities to launch their imaginations.*

Above: Tots can dress up like a penguin, slide down "ice," and build a nest with a toy chick in Polar Play Zone's penguin playscape.

Polar Play Zone

As part of the Oceanarium renovation, Shedd's exhibit designers turned their attention to an under-utilized area—the cavernous underwater viewing gallery—to create a permanent exhibit just for children, where they could play, splash, pretend and learn.

Polar Play Zone features kid-favorite animals: beluga whales, dolphins, sea otters and penguins. There are also lots of things to touch and engaging activities that will accommodate different learning styles. For example, a theme of polar opposites neatly relates northern hemisphere marine mammals to southern hemisphere penguins and offers comparisons of big and little, fast and slow, shallow and deep, leaping and diving, helping kids to understand how the animals live in their icy environments.

The fully accessible exhibit starts with a touch pool filled with live bumpy sea stars and prickly sea urchins, and a water-play table with movable model tide-pool animals. The next stop is a real-life penguin exhibit mirrored by a polar "playscape" where kids can slip into penguin costumes, romp on rubberized "rocks" and "ice," build nests with big pretend eggs and even feed lifelike toy fish to plush penguin chicks. From there, kids can make the imaginative leap to being polar explorers in a 15-foot yellow submarine. Equipped with instruments, a periscope and even a robotic arm for exploring rocks on the nearby "seafloor," the submarine is a kid magnet that attracts parents too.

4
PART FOUR

THE WORLD'S
AQUARIUM

Far left: These Magellanic penguin chicks hatched at Shedd. They are native to South America's chilly southern tip, not the southern polar region.

Left: The slow-moving panther chameleon is endemic to Madagascar's rapidly disappearing forests.

Opposite: A Pacific white-sided dolphin enjoys a training session. Shedd's larger animals all learn behaviors that help with their hands-on care, including exams.

Animals connect us to the living world, inspiring us to make a difference. They are our most eloquent ambassadors for conservation. The beluga whales, Pacific white-sided dolphins, sea otters and California sea lions in the Oceanarium speak to the importance of maintaining a healthy ocean ecosystem. The spectral array of creatures in Wild Reef is an awe-inspiring example of the irreplaceable biodiversity that hangs in the balance as coral reefs throughout the tropics face a host of threats. Closer to home, side-by-side displays of native Great Lakes fishes and aggressive invasive species are a call to informed action to protect the world's largest body of fresh water—and the aquatic environment 42 million people depend on—from ecological disaster.

Superior care of all the animals in the collection is the top priority at Shedd. The aquarium was designed with unprecedented behind-the-scenes space for animal care, a standard carried on in the Oceanarium, Wild Reef and the full-service animal hospital. The treatment of aquatic animals is the final frontier in veterinary medicine. Rapid advances in knowledge and technology have made possible wellness checks as well as critical care for animals of every stripe and blood type, from beluga whales to seadragons, and increasingly for invertebrates.

Our animals inspire people in different ways: to help clean a beach; to contact a legislator; to volunteer; to become a marine biologist; to visit again and again with a favorite fish. Whether for their beauty, size, personality, rarity, longevity, or some indefinable magnetism, certain animals through the years have become favorites with the public and staff alike. They are our inspirations.

Adopting Granddad

AUSTRALIAN LUNGFISH (Neoceratodus forsteri)

Australian lungfish are native to the Mary and Burnett Rivers in Queensland, in northeastern Australia. Lungfish, which possess a single primitive lung as well as gills, are among the few fishes that can breathe air. This allows them to survive seasonal changes in the level and quality of their shallow habitats by noisily gulping air every 30 to 60 minutes.

Australian lungfish have been around for 100 million years. Shedd Aquarium's eldest Australian lungfish isn't quite that old, but his arrival in May 1933 makes him the senior resident in the building and the longest-lived individual of his species. In fact, he is the oldest fish in any aquarium or zoo in the world.

Director Walter H. Chute wanted an exceptional display of colorful and unusual fishes to attract some of the 10 million visitors expected to attend the Century of Progress World's Fair just steps from the aquarium. In March 1933 he sent a letter to the director of the aquarium in Sydney to tell him that two Shedd collectors would arrive aboard the steamer *Mariposa* on April 27. He attached a wish list of animals and emphasized that Shedd was especially interested in acquiring a pair of lungfish.

On May 6, when the collectors departed Sydney aboard the *Mariposa*, they had with them a prized collection of Australian fishes, including two lungfish. The ship headed to Honolulu, where two other Shedd collectors were waiting with containers of triggerfish, puffers and other Hawaiian reef fishes. Two-and-a-half weeks later, the boat docked in Los Angeles, where Shedd's railroad car, the *Nautilus*, was ready to be loaded. The collection arrived in Chicago on May 27, right

around the opening of the World's Fair. Granddad and his mate, who lived until 1980, were the first of their kind on exhibit in the United States.

Shedd did not acquire more lungfish until 1994, when the University of Queensland and Australia's Sea World donated five young lungfish to join Granddad. Because of their small population, restricted range and degraded breeding habitat, lungfish are considered a threatened species in Australia, and the government rarely allows them to be exported. These youngsters, at the time estimated to be between 8 and 10 years old, were donated to the aquarium to establish a breeding program in the United States.

Under this breeding program, Shedd researchers have tried re-creating the subtle seasonal changes in water temperature and pH that can put this species in a spawning mood in the wild. Researchers are also studying additional habitat requirements. Little is known about lungfish reproductive biology, and to date, the fish have not bred. But with this species' reputation for longevity, there appears to be time for Shedd's program to succeed.

Chico: A Shedd Favorite

AMAZON RIVER DOLPHIN (Inia geoffrensis)

Found in the Amazon and Orinoco river systems of South America, these freshwater dolphins never enter the ocean. Amazon river dolphins use echolocation to navigate, find food and avoid obstacles in murky rain forest rivers. They use their long rostrums to poke the river bottom for mud-dwelling fishes, crayfish and other food, which they grab with their sharp teeth.

If Shedd Aquarium ever had a mascot, it was Chico, a freshwater dolphin from Peru. His 16-year stay at Shedd set a longevity record for an Amazon river dolphin, or "boto," for many years.

While traveling in Florida in 1965, then-aquarium director William P. Braker came across a 2-year-old dolphin kept in a tiny holding tank by an animal dealer. Braker quickly arranged to have the dolphin shipped to Shedd. When Chico arrived, he was 4 feet long and weighed 80 pounds. He grew into a 6-foot-3, 225-pound adult. Chico enjoyed a 13,500-gallon pool, "trained" staff members to play games with him as they walked by and drew 4,100 aquarium guests to his 18th birthday party in October 1981.

Chico had a funny, Muppet-like face, with a long rostrum (beak), button eyes and a prominent melon (the echolocating organ in his forehead) that he could scrunch back, pushing the corners of his natural dolphin grin even higher. Freshwater dolphins like Chico have poor vision, so they rely on echolocation to navigate their native shallow, sediment-filled rivers. Like other dolphins and whales, Chico generated sound waves that would bounce back from an object and tell him its size, shape and distance.

True to his species, Chico was also a deliberate swimmer who seldom rushed anywhere. Some guests, familiar with the athleticism of bottlenose and other marine dolphins, worried that Chico was ill. The aquarium took pains to let everyone know that his low-speed behavior was perfectly normal.

Chico was cared for his entire time at Shedd by senior aquarist Howard Karsner, who developed activity sessions that combined feeding, a daily exam, exercise and play. When Chico presented his tail, Karsner gently swiped a soft-bristled brush over the flukes. Eventually Karsner would toss the brush into the water, and Chico would retrieve it to have the rest of his body brushed.

Although river dolphins—especially males—are not very social, Chico enjoyed the time staff divers spent in the water with him, playing tag and other games. Chico lived until March 1982.

Octopuses: The Long and Short of Them

GIANT PACIFIC OCTOPUS (Enteroctopus dofleini)

The giant Pacific octopus can turn its light brown skin to red, black, or orange in less than a second with chromatophores, special skin cells filled with pigments. Arms outstretched, an adult measures 16 feet across and weighs between 50 and 90 pounds. Newly hatched young are the size of a grain of rice.

The octopus has a brief life span. A September 1930 Shedd press release announcing a collecting expedition to Key West noted, "The early death of the octopi, which usually die after a day in captivity, has troubled aquarium directors for years. But with special apparatus and modern appliances the Aquarium hopes to keep the native species for a long time." Soon after, an American octopus at Shedd would set a record among northern aquariums by living five and a half months.

Director Walter H. Chute kept meticulous notes on environmental and nutritional requirements, as well as medical treatments, for the hundreds of species on display. But in the case of octopuses, most filtration technology at the time could not meet the animals' water-quality requirements for long-term survival.

Even with today's computerized life-support systems, however, aquariums can't change the fact that octopuses die soon after reproducing. A hormone is released that causes the animal to stop eating; the female stays alive only long enough to tend her eggs until they hatch. The giant Pacific octopuses that Shedd displays typically live about two years. What makes this short lifespan all the more frustrating to the octopus keepers is that these animals are smart and trainable.

Just like marine mammals, octopuses need behavioral enrichment—interesting things to do—to stay healthy and happy. For an octopus, that might be a prey puzzle, such as a container the creature must open to reach fish, crab, or other food hidden inside.

Prey puzzles provide natural problem-solving activities and allow aquarium guests to see the animal in action as a hunter. Shedd's giant Pacific octopuses are given both snap-lid and screw-top plastic containers filled with fish. It's hard to say who is more engaged, the octopus retrieving its treat or the guests watching.

Opposite: A young Deadeye (center) swims with two other tarpons collected in 1935 in this archival photo.

Right: Though nearly blind from an accident that occurred during the middle of her life, Deadeye lived at Shedd for 63 years. Her story was one of the highlights of presentations in the Caribbean Reef exhibit.

Deadeye: Shedd's Silver Queen

TARPON (Megalops atlanticus)

Tarpons mostly convene in tropical waters, although they can venture as far north as Cape Cod, Massachusetts, in the summer. They hunt at night, catching shrimp, mullet and other surface-feeding fishes in their large upturned mouths. The powerful 5- to 8-foot fish are a favorite with anglers because they will fight and leap until exhausted.

Deadeye, Shedd's venerable, nearly blind Atlantic tarpon, spent 63 years at the aquarium, 27 of them in the Caribbean Reef exhibit. At the time of her death in 1998, she was the oldest Atlantic tarpon in a zoological collection.

Deadeye's story involves one of Shedd's most dramatic collecting trips. In August 1935 an aquarium crew was in Key West collecting fishes for the saltwater exhibits. They were living aboard the *Nautilus*, a Pullman railroad car customized for transporting fishes. On September 2, the day the *Nautilus* was to head home, one of the 20th century's worst hurricanes smashed through the Keys, killing at least 423 people and wiping out everything in its path—including the railroad track that connected the

islands to the mainland. The Shedd staffers and their fishes were unharmed. But they were stranded for two months until the ferry landing at Fort Lauderdale was rebuilt and the *Nautilus* could be removed by boat.

While they waited, the crew endured another hurricane, equipment breakdowns and the challenge of keeping a variety of fishes and invertebrates alive in the railroad car's holding tanks and in "live cars" that were submerged offshore. But the crew continued to collect a few more species on their wish list, including some small tarpons. The *Nautilus* finally rolled into Chicago on November 9, and Deadeye and at least two others became the first Atlantic tarpons on display in a public aquarium.

Deadeye didn't acquire her name until 1959, when she survived a near-fatal accident. Tarpons are jumpy by nature, and she became spooked during routine exhibit maintenance. Instinctively, the powerful fish leaped from her Gallery 1 exhibit into another tank, then another, and finally landed, thrashing, on the floor. She lost half her scales and most of her vision. Aquarists spent more than six months nursing her back to health.

Fortunately, Deadeye could still navigate, thanks to her lateral lines, the sensory organs that a fish has along its head and sides. When the Caribbean Reef opened in 1971, she was among the first residents of the 90,000-gallon exhibit, and she became one of the most popular animals. Because of her limited vision, though, she occasionally swam into other fishes and exhibit rockwork. One night in 1998, she wedged herself between some artificial corals and was badly injured as she wriggled out. This time, the aquarists and veterinarians weren't able to save her.

Sport fishermen call the tarpon the "silver king," and Deadeye was Shedd's "silver queen." Her remarkable longevity is a credit to her tenacity and to the many dedicated aquarists who cared for her during her six decades at the aquarium.

Above: Lindy is one of several neon tetras in the lower central part of this photo from Shedd's 1936 annual report.

Right: While native to the Amazon, most neon tetras in the pet trade are bred on fish farms in Southeast Asia.

Lindy, the Flying Fish

NEON TETRA (Paracheirodon innesi)

Neon tetras live in the deeply shaded black waters of smaller rivers in the Amazon basin. Their brilliant blue side stripes function like neon signs, reflecting rays of light to enable them to find each other in their murky habitat. The tiny fish then band together, gaining safety in numbers by schooling.

Given how common neon tetras are in home aquariums, it's hard to imagine the excitement that was generated by the arrival of one tiny tetra on July 13, 1936. But Lindy was the first neon tetra ever displayed in this country. Thousands of people lined up on the front steps of the aquarium to get in to see the 1-inch fish.

Perhaps it was the novel way in which Lindy arrived at the aquarium that drew the crowds and reporters. Lindy had been collected in Peru and was part of a shipment of fishes that traveled by boat to Germany. Named for aviation hero Charles A. Lindbergh, Lindy was the first fish to fly from Germany to Chicago.

Lindy was one of six neon tetras sent to Shedd on the German airship *Hindenburg*. Four of the fish died of exposure to the cold during the flight across the Atlantic, and a fifth died in New York. The tough little survivor was transferred to a plane for the final leg of the trip to Chicago's Midway Airport.

When aquarium director Walter H. Chute met Lindy, he noted sadly to reporters, "It's very weak." After three days of intensive care in Shedd's fish hospital, however, Lindy rallied and went on to dazzle guests in the balanced aquarium room. Lindy was joined not long afterward by eight more neon tetras from the German aquarium—sent less conspicuously by steamer.

Stout Guinness's Weigh-in

ALLIGATOR SNAPPING TURTLE (Macrochelys temminckii)

Weighing up to 250 pounds, alligator snappers are the largest of the North American freshwater turtles. Populations have plummeted throughout the species' range, which extends from the Deep South to southern Illinois and Indiana. Because they are large and lethargic, alligator snappers are easy targets and have been hunted extensively for meat. They have also suffered from degradation and destruction of their habitats, which include lakes, ponds, swamps and the deep channels of large river systems. Although they are not federally protected, alligator snappers are listed as endangered in many states or threatened, as in Illinois. Large ones are extremely rare, both in the wild and in aquariums.

Few animals at Shedd have the drawing power of a big alligator snapping turtle doing nothing. One-hundred-pound Guinness is no exception. (The name was inspired by a photo from the turtle's donor showing the reptile next to a 16-ounce can of the Irish brew for size comparison.) What is it that fascinates people about the algae-covered turtle? Certainly his size, but perhaps it's also the anticipation of . . . some movement. More than any alligator snapper before him at Shedd, Guinness doesn't disappoint.

Twice a week, Guinness has a training session that is similar to the dolphins' daily activities and uses the same techniques. On a visual cue, the turtle swims to a ramp that can be extended into his habitat and lumbers out to get a reward of herring, capelin, or mice dropped

into his mouth. He receives about a half-pound of food each session. Not surprisingly, Guinness has learned to anticipate the sessions, which combine training with his regular feeding schedule. Often he's waiting at the door when the aquarists open the back of the habitat.

Training provides animals with physical exercise and mental stimulation. It also gets them accustomed to interacting with staff members in ways that make medical care easier. In Guinness's case, he is walking onto a platform on which he can be weighed regularly, an important aspect of his health care. In the past, such behemoths might only be weighed every few years because hoisting them out of the water was an ordeal for all parties involved. For Guinness, the exercise is just another feeding session.

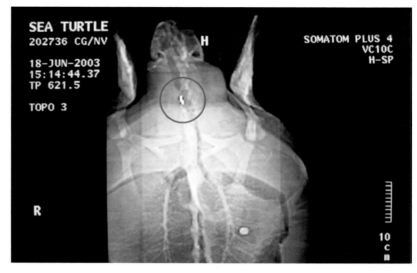

Banking on Nickel

GREEN SEA TURTLE (Chelonia mydas)

Greens are the largest of the hard-shelled sea turtles, with adults weighing from 300 to 500 pounds. They range throughout the world's tropical oceans, grazing on turtle grass and other marine vegetation. Their survival is threatened by dangerous fishing practices, coastal development and fibropapilloma, a crippling virus afflicting green turtles worldwide.

Shedd's green sea turtle, Nickel, took to the Caribbean Reef exhibit as if she'd never lived anywhere else. On her first day in the 90,000-gallon habitat in July 2003, the 124-pound turtle swam among the hundreds of fishes, ate a hearty meal of romaine lettuce and found a cozy place to nap between two elkhorn corals. Only a few guests noticed that Nickel's swimming posture was a bit off balance—head down, rump up.

Five years earlier, a marine biologist had spotted the sea turtle floating among mangroves along Florida's Gulf Coast. Thin and weak, she couldn't move her hind feet to swim. A deep gash ran from the rear edge to the center of her carapace, or upper shell, unmistakably a wound from a motorboat propeller.

She was taken to Clearwater Marine Aquarium for treatment. Yet despite months of rehabilitation, the turtle continued to have problems controlling her buoyancy and using her paddlelike hind feet, which serve as rudders and brakes. Permanently injured, she could not be returned to the ocean.

Working with the Florida Fish and Wildlife Conservation Commission, Shedd welcomed the turtle in April 2003. Shedd veterinarians gave the friendly, easygoing turtle a thorough medical exam that included radiographs at Shedd's animal healthcare center and a CT scan at a local hospital. She had suffered some internal damage from the boat strike, but nothing life-threatening. What

alarmed the doctors was a round image—a coin—in her esophagus. Using a small retrieval tool with an endoscope, vets removed a nickel from the turtle's throat. The problem was solved, and the turtle had a name.

Nickel will always have buoyancy problems, but her hind legs have gotten stronger with exercise, and she easily dives to the floor of the 13-foot-deep reef exhibit for her food. She has regular training sessions, just like the whales and dolphins, and she's learned to come to, or "target" on, a yellow hand-held buoy. Some-times a trainer will stand outside the Caribbean Reef holding a yellow oval to the window for her to target on. (Yes, the animals can see through the glass.) Nickel has also learned to swim into a mesh sling at the top of the exhibit, a move that makes her wellness exams a lot easier for her and the veterinary team.

Nickel is one of only a few rehabilitated sea turtles on permanent display in the United States. Her presence serves as a reminder that the way we use—or abuse—wildlife areas has lasting consequences.

Right: When Mari came to Shedd as a tiny pup, she was bottle-fed a puree of clam, squid, half-and-half and vitamins every four hours.

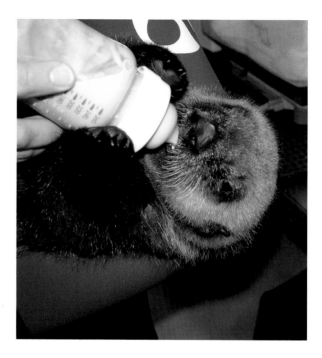

Sea Otter R&R:
Rescue and Rearing
SEA OTTER (Enhydra lutris)

Unlike other marine mammals, sea otters don't have a thick layer of blubber to keep them warm in the cold Pacific Ocean. They do, however, have the densest fur of any mammal, which they diligently groom and fluff with air to hold in body heat. Pups must gobble the daily equivalent of one-third their body weight to survive and grow, while adults eat nearly one-quarter of their body weight each day to fuel their high metabolism. That's about 15 pounds of sea urchins, mussels, clams, crabs, squid and fish for a 60-pound animal.

When an orphaned or abandoned sea otter pup in Alaska needs a home, U.S. Fish and Wildlife Service (FWS) officials call Shedd Aquarium. Shedd's reputation for expertise in raising these high-risk, high-maintenance babies grew out of a disaster.

In mid-March 1989 the aquarium received confirmation that a permit to collect otters in Prince William Sound, Alaska, for the new Oceanarium had been approved. A week later, a FWS official called to say that the permit would be delayed. The tanker *Exxon Valdez* had run aground in Prince William Sound, coating 1,100 miles of coast with 11 million gallons of crude oil. Tens of thousands of animals—fishes, eagles, seabirds and sea otters—were dead; thousands more needed immediate intensive treatment to survive.

Shedd sent members of its animal care staff to the sea otter rescue center in the harbor town of Valdez. There, they assisted in cleaning oiled otters and tending to recovering ones around the clock. At the end of their stay, they were asked by center officials how many otters Shedd would like. FWS was releasing rehabilitated adult otters into unaffected areas of the sound, but the service was also looking for qualified aquariums and zoos to provide homes to a small number of orphaned or abandoned pups (ranging from a few weeks to a few months old) that would not survive in the wild.

That's how Kenai, Nikishka, Nuka and Chenik—all given Alaska place names—came to Shedd. At the time, the Oceanarium was still under construction, so they lived in a double habitat in the galleries, the first sea otters on display in an inland North American aquarium.

Within a year, FWS called to see if Shedd could take a 1-month-old pup found stranded along

Left: Shedd's pioneering training program for sea otters has been a model for other aquariums that care for these high-spirited animals.

Above: Kenai was a pup orphaned soon after the Exxon Valdez *oil spill in 1989. She is also shown in the foreground, left.*

Kachemak Bay. Wildlife officials speculated that the 6-pound pup had been separated from her mother during a storm. The newcomer, Kachemak, came to Shedd, and by the time the Oceanarium opened in 1991, Shedd had a rollicking group of young sea otters.

Then in 2003, another pup, Mari, was brought to a wildlife facility by a kayaker who didn't know that the young otter floating alone in a kelp bed had actually been safely "parked" there by her mom, who was off hunting. Once removed, Mari could not be put back, so FWS sent her to Shedd. Kiana, who arrived in 2005, had been in real trouble. A group of recreational boaters kept an eye on the tiny, screaming pup all day, but evidently knew not to interfere immediately. When they were convinced that the mother wasn't returning, they called wildlife officials, who rescued the pup.

With each new pup that comes to Shedd, the marine mammals staffers kick into high gear for several months of round-the-clock caregiving in a behind-the-scenes otter nursery. Every four hours the pup is bottle-fed. Then it is bathed in a child's splash pool (and given lessons on how to float and swim), towel dried and groomed with a hair dryer to fluff its insulating fur. The pup sleeps until it is time to eat again. In 2009, the Oceanarium was renovated to include expanded nursery facilities and a new, 1,000-gallon "pup pool."

More than 20 years after the oil spill, three of the original 13 adopted pups—now super-seniors in sea otter terms—are still going strong at several North American aquariums. They include Nuka, who moved to the Seattle Aquarium in 2001 in exchange for Shedd's only male otter, Yaku, and Kenai, still the matriarch of the Oceanarium's otter cove.

While she often opts out of playtime, Kenai enjoys her training sessions and the food rewards that go along with them. Sometimes she and Kachemak take a time-out in the pup pool from the high-energy antics of the younger animals. While Kenai never had a pup, she played surrogate mom to Kiana. The now-adult Kiana still allows Kenai to pull her around like a pup, evidence of the bond between the oldest and youngest of Shedd's rescued sea otters.

Safe Haven for Seahorses

SEAHORSES (Family Syngnathidae)

Seahorses are the best-known members of a wildly diverse family of fishes that also includes seadragons, pipefishes and pipehorses. Their unifying characteristics are a long, tube-shaped mouth; a slender body encased in bony armor or rings; small, delicate fins; and a unique reproductive strategy in which the female deposits eggs on or in the male's body for incubation, and the male gives birth to the offspring. These fishes are also masters of camouflage, whether changing their body color, growing skin filaments to mimic seaweed, or swimming vertically to blend in among seagrass fronds.

"The seahorse is without doubt the most popular exhibit in the aquarium," Shedd's director noted as 100 of the delicate equine-faced fish went into a new exhibit. "The seahorse intrigues all new visitors, and although some people come back regularly, they never seem to get tired of watching it."

While this sentiment could have applied to the animals in Shedd Aquarium's wildly popular "Seahorse Symphony," a special exhibit that ran from 1998 through 2003, the words were actually spoken by Walter H. Chute in 1935. In the 1930s, Shedd exhibited lined seahorses (*Hippocampus erectus*) from the North Atlantic coast. At the time, this species was becoming scarce because a blight was wiping out its eelgrass

habitat. Today seahorses face different threats: destruction of their coastal habitats, including coral reefs, mangroves and seagrass beds; hunting to make trinkets and souvenirs; and overfishing to meet the demand for dried seahorses used in traditional Chinese medicine. In the 1990s, 24 million seahorses were taken from the wild each year, 95 percent of them for medicinal use.

In 1998 Shedd formed a conservation partnership with Project Seahorse, an international conservation organization. From the original focus on seahorses and the people who depend on them for their livelihoods, the partnership has expanded to encompass the conservation and sustainable use of the world's coastal marine ecosystems.

Fauna and Flora (CITES)—a first for marine fishes.

With Shedd's support, Project Seahorse has created teams of Filipino scientists and community workers that help subsistence fishing villages set up marine protected areas, or MPAs, within their waters. MPAs are scientifically determined and locally agreed-upon no-fishing zones. These refuges, which include premium feeding and breeding habitats, enable depleted fish stocks to rebound, often within three years. As the fish population expands within an MPA, it overflows into the designated fishing grounds, restoring resources for traditional livelihoods. The community-managed MPAs have proven so successful for fishes and fishermen alike that Project Seahorse has already lent its expertise in establishing 33 such areas throughout the Philippines. And more communities are asking for them.

Meanwhile at Shedd, aquarists have developed better techniques for feeding the young. They have also fine-tuned the nursery environment, leading to greater success in raising seahorses for display in the galleries and at sister aquariums.

Since the 1930s charismatic seahorses have intrigued Shedd Aquarium's guests. In return, Shedd continues to inspire its guests to help protect these magnificent creatures.

Together, Shedd and Project Seahorse have helped seahorse fishing families in the Philippines develop alternative livelihoods, including ecotourism and handicrafts (with products sold at Shedd and other aquariums). They have also provided high school tuition for fishermen's children while involving them in marine conservation apprenticeships.

Shedd hosted a workshop for aquarium and zoo professionals from around the world on the care, breeding and educational display of seahorses, and biologists from Shedd and Project Seahorse coauthored the first manual for seahorse husbandry. In 2004 Shedd assisted Project Seahorse in gaining worldwide protection for seahorses under the Convention on International Trade in Endangered Species of Wild

Bubba: A Symbol of Hope

QUEENSLAND GROUPER (Epinephelus lanceolatus)

Queensland groupers—not sharks, as most people assume—are the top predators on Indo-Pacific reefs. They can reach lengths of 8 feet and weigh nearly 900 pounds. For three years, Bubba, a 5-foot, 154-pound Queensland grouper, ruled Shedd's 400,000-gallon Wild Reef habitat (also home to 20 sharks). But Bubba's real renown came from being the first fish known to have received chemotherapy to treat malignant tumors. Subsequently, he became an oddly lovable symbol of hope for cancer patients across the country, especially the youngest ones.

Bubba arrived at Shedd in 1987 as a 10-inch youngster, swimming in a small cooler that was left at the receptionist's desk. Most likely, his owner realized too late that this fast-growing fish would become larger than a home aquarium could accommodate. (Shedd urges hobbyists to know what they're getting into before buying an animal.)

Bubba eventually occupied a 13,500-gallon Pacific reef habitat in Gallery 2. Always interested in the humans around him, the affable fish was a favorite of guests and staff members alike. In 1999, construction for the Amazon Rising exhibit began in Bubba's gallery, and the magnificent 4-foot-long fish was moved to a large reserve pool until another new exhibit, Wild Reef, was completed in 2003. Bubba was going to be one of the stars of its high-profile shark habitat.

Before that happened, though, aquarists noticed pimplelike bumps on Bubba's head. When antibiotics didn't heal the growths, the vets performed a biopsy. The results were negative, but a second biopsy indicated a malignant tumor. In 2002, Shedd doctors, assisted by an outside veterinary surgeon and veterinary oncologist, removed the affected tissue and injected chemotherapy treatments around the wound. But the cancer came back. In March 2003 the veterinary team removed a broader, deeper section of tissue from Bubba's head. The vets covered the wound with pigskin tissue to speed healing and once again injected a chemotherapy agent around the edges of the cut-out area. Seven months later Bubba got a clean bill of health and was moved into the central Wild Reef habitat.

The unique cancer survivor earned an entry in Wikipedia and a commemorative tile bearing his name in the oncology department of Hope Children's Hospital in Oak Lawn, Illinois. His death of age-related causes in 2006 was noted in *Time* magazine as well as in the scientific journal *Nature*.

Hand-raising Kayavak

BELUGA WHALE (Delphinapterus leucas)

Belugas are found in coastal waters throughout the Arctic—off Scandinavia, Alaska, Canada and Siberia—as well as in the St. Lawrence River and Hudson Bay. They are small whales, ranging from 12 to 16 feet long and weighing between 1,500 and 3,300 pounds, with up to 6 inches of blubber to keep them warm. Belugas produce thousands of sounds in their nasal passages that they broadcast through their blowholes, including high-pitched whistles, squeals, clicks and chirps.

Born August 3, 1999, Kayavak was Shedd Aquarium's first successful beluga birth. Her first birthday—complete with cake and candle—was a milestone for everyone involved with her care.

As the first calf of Immiayuk, one of Shedd's two original beluga whales, Kayavak's odds of survival had been poor. Immi was an inexperienced mother, and Kayavak was an independent baby. Animal care team members exhaled in relief when mother and daughter bonded and the calf started nursing. Immi turned out to be an excellent mom, and Kayavak mimicked her every move, to the delight of the staff and guests.

On December 26, 1999, Immi suddenly became ill and died. Her death stunned the staff; the beloved 14-year-old whale had been in excellent health. Tests revealed that Immi had died from erysipelas, a fast-acting bacterial infection that overwhelms the organ systems. The condition also affects cetaceans in the wild.

To better understand this disease, Shedd later hosted an international erysipelas workshop for aquarium professionals. The collaborative research presented new ways of preventing and treating the infection, helping the aquarium and zoo community cope with this devastating disease.

Not quite 5 months old, Kayavak was still nursing when her mother died. But she was just old enough to digest solid food. After much consultation, the animal care team decided to wean Kayavak since her chances of survival would be much better on nutritious fish than artificial formula. The calf was too small to be with the adult belugas, so for months she lived in the Oceanarium's medical pool with 24-hour care and attention from trainers and volunteers. She played with a variety of children's pool toys, often with her wet-suited friends. Gradually Kayavak was introduced to the adult female belugas, and when another calf was born in 2000, she had a playmate of her own species.

Kayavak is an adolescent now and, as one of the stars of Shedd's aquatic show, she makes a big splash. Watch closely and you'll see that she seems to hold dual citizenship—in the belugas' world and in the human one, too.

Homegrown Belugas

Kayavak, Qannik (who moved from Shedd in 2007), Bella, Miki and, most recently, a yet-to-be-named calf were born in the Oceanarium, the results of a cooperative beluga breeding program involving Shedd and five other North American aquariums and zoos. The nearly 40 beluga whales living at these facilities are considered one population, and from time to time individuals are moved between locations to make the most of reproductive opportunities. This shifting among groups is similar to the fluid social groups belugas form in the wild.

The carefully administered breeding program ensures that the whales live in genetically diverse groups. Age, previous reproductive success, mothering skills and a facility's capacity for additional animals also figure into the matchmaking equation. Since the breeding program was initiated in 1995, there have been 21 successful births among the participating zoological facilities, with one or two calves born each year.

A total of nine beluga calves

Opposite: Five-week-old Miki, right, swims with mom Mauyak, center, and Naya, another female beluga who has helped raise most of Shedd's calves.

Left: Three-day-old Bella peeks over mom Puiji to check out a diver cleaning the pool. Since calves sense their mother's trust in the people around them, they aren't afraid of divers and trainers.

Below: Puiji's newest calf, shown at 1 month old swimming with his mom, was born in December 2009. His weight doubled—to 325 pounds—in two months. "Babysitter" Naya is in the background.

have been born at Shedd since 1998. In aquariums, as in the wild, the average survival rate is about 50 percent, with calf survival increasing dramatically among older, more experienced mothers. The cooperative program has led to more successful births through shared expertise and a growing database on beluga reproductive and neonatal biology.

Above: Striped zebra shark pups live up to the species' common name. The dark bands later turn into spots.

Right: Tail biting is normal courtship behavior among zebra sharks. Here, Cleo is the focus of Andre's advances.

Cleo: Super Mom

ZEBRA SHARK (Stegostoma fasciatum)

Zebra sharks do not have to swim to breathe. By day they rest on the sandy reef floor with their mouths open and powerful throat muscles pumping water across their gills, often facing into the current to get more oxygenated water. By night they search for food. Slim and sinuous, zebra sharks can squirm into crevices and small caves in the coral. Then, like vacuum cleaners, they suck in snails, clams, crabs, shrimps and small fishes, crushing them with their powerful teeth.

A zebra shark is easy to identify by its super-long caudal (or tail) fin, which is fully half the fish's 6½- to 8-foot length. Individuals can be identified by their dark brown spot patterns, which are as unique as our fingerprints.

"Zebra" seems a misnomer for a shark with spots—until you see the striped pups. And the aquarists who tend the zebra sharks in Wild Reef have seen a lot of pups. As of early 2010, 87 zebra shark pups have hatched at Shedd. Eighty-six of them came from eggs laid by Cleo. In the aquarium world, that's a record. Cleo arrived in 2003 from the waters off northeastern Australia, joining several other zebras in Shedd's Wild Reef.

Zebra shark eggs are big—about 7 inches long, 3 inches wide and 2 inches thick—and have tufts of hair-like fibers called adhesive tendrils at one end. As the mother shark lays her eggs, she swims circles around vertical reef formations to snag the fibers and safely anchor the cases.

At Shedd, the eggs are collected and placed in a circular tub filled with salt water. They are either suspended from a monofilament line or kept in a floating basket, and once a month they're checked with ultrasound. After about five months of incubation, a foot-long pup—dark brown with bold white or pale yellow vertical bands—wriggles out of each egg ready to hunt and hide in the nursery tub. As the pups grow, the dark areas break up into spots on an expanding light background.

Shedd raises Cleo's offspring in reserve pools for three to five months before distributing them to other aquariums and zoos for display. Cleo's kids have been seen in at least 16 other U.S. aquariums. But Cleo isn't the only mom in Wild Reef. Vera, Shedd's other adult female zebra, hatched her first pup in November 2009.

Biff and Otis: No More Poached Salmon

CALIFORNIA SEA LION (Zalophus californianus)

If you hear one before you see it, you'll understand how sea lions got their name. The mountainous males can emit thunderous roars to defend their territories. For all their heft, however, sea lions are sleek under water, swimming 15 to 20 mph and making tight turns to catch their prey: rockfish, flatfish, hake—and, yes, salmon.

It was a case of federally protected marine mammals chowing down on federally endangered fish. Biff and Otis were among a group of California sea lions who had found an easy meal of spawning Chinook salmon along the Bonneville Dam on Oregon's Columbia River. The sea lions were taking such a toll on the critically endangered fish that wildlife biologists relocated them. To monitor their whereabouts and eating habits, veterinarians branded large identification numbers on the sea lions' backs.

(The procedure was done using anesthetics, and the sea lions were given a medical exam before they were released.)

When Shedd acquired sea lions C 507 and C 700 (named for Columbia), their numbers were almost up; they'd been identified as "problem animals." As a last resort, wildlife officials slated them for permanent removal. That's usually a death sentence, but the federal government and the marine mammal display community collaborated to find 700 (now Biff), 507 (Otis) and several other salmon poachers new homes at zoos and aquariums.

Today, the salmon are safer, the sea lions are saved, and Shedd has welcomed two fantastic marine mammals to its Oceanarium sea lion habitat.

Iguanas on a Rocky Road to Survival
WEST INDIAN ROCK IGUANAS (Genus Cyclura)

The blue iguana (*Cyclura lewisi*) is found only on Grand Cayman Island, which, despite its name, is just a dot on a map between Cuba and Jamaica. The Grand Cayman blue iguana is one of nine species of rock iguanas, large and often colorful lizards that are unique to the West Indies. All nine species are endangered. Shedd Aquarium is active in conservation programs for two species, at home and in the field.

When Shedd's pair of Grand Cayman blue iguanas moved into a new 1,200-square-foot tropical island habitat in 2005, fewer than two dozen of their wild brethren were still skittering through the underbrush on Grand Cayman. At the time, blue iguanas were the most endangered lizards in the world, having been heavily preyed on by dogs and cats, hit by cars and pushed out of their habitats by development.

Today their foothold is a little firmer, thanks to a successful breeding and release program by the Blue Iguana Recovery Program (BIRP), part of the National Trust for the Cayman Islands. So far, about 350 blue iguanas raised at BIRP facilities have been released into protected areas on the rocky island—about one-third the number needed for a healthy, self-sustaining population.

This small group is vulnerable to natural and manmade disasters, so BIRP established a second population in the United States as a hedge against extinction. It currently numbers about three dozen animals distributed among 13 aquariums and zoos, including Shedd.

These lizards are part of a Species Survival Plan (SSP), one of 116 such programs of the Association of Zoos and Aquariums to ensure the long-term survival of selected endangered species by maintaining genetically diverse populations at member facilities and carefully managing cooperative breeding programs. SSPs also involve research, public education, reintroduction where protected habitats exist and field conservation projects for wild populations. The rock iguana SSP, which counts the blue iguana as one of its highest priorities, was established in 1996. Shedd is among the original participants. So far, the U.S. partners have had slim breeding success. Each spring, Shedd saw energetic mating behavior between its iguanas, Marley and Eleanor, but no eggs. Hopes ended with Eleanor's death in 2010. Marley, an impressive individual, continues to fulfill his role as

an ambassador for his species, helping to draw public attention to the blue iguana's plight.

Since 1994, Shedd has also conducted field research on the Bahamian rock iguana, *C. cychlura*, on Andros Island and on the Exuma island chain. Much of the research has been aided by volunteer citizen scientists who each year join Shedd's iguana biologist, Dr. Chuck Knapp, aboard the aquarium's research vessel, the R/V *Coral Reef II*, to collect data on the lizards from some of the Bahamas' most remote and rugged islands.

These long-term observations have helped piece together the elusive lizards' natural histories, including feeding and nesting adaptations unique to the Andros population. In 2009, the Bahamian government expanded a national park to encompass the Andros iguana's critical habitat, using data collected over 10 years by Shedd's research team to help redraw the boundaries.

Meanwhile, Shedd is addressing emerging physi-ological and behavioral problems associated with the lizards' exposure to increasing numbers of tourists—problems that could threaten the long-term survival of these endangered animals. (Some tourists, for example, are offering junk food to them.) This study includes comparing blood chemistries and stress hormones in different iguana populations. The results will help wildlife biologists in the Bahamas create management policies to better protect the iguanas and their habitats.

Shedd's boat is a familiar sight to the residents of the "settlements" along the coasts of these islands. As critical as the field studies are, the educational programs that Shedd brings to the local schools and community centers are also important. They encourage pride in and stewardship of each island's unique iguana species. Shedd sponsored a youth soccer club on Andros, whose members were so inspired by one of biologist Knapp's presentations that they named their team the Iguanas.

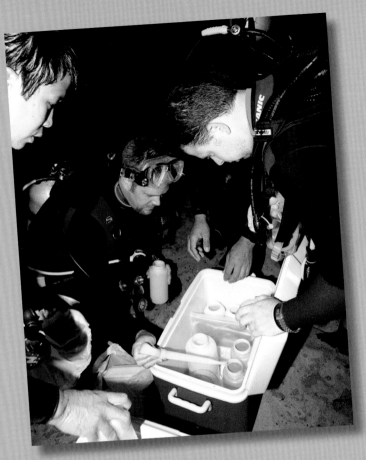

Coral Conservation

Corals are the building blocks of the reef ecosystem and the foundation of Shedd's Wild Reef exhibit. Wild Reef is home to nearly 60 species of live corals. Most of these colonial animals bask under bright metal halide lamps in a 6,000-gallon exhibit, and nearly all of them are homegrown.

This last point is important. More than 2,000 species of corals are at risk of extinction, including Caribbean elkhorn (*Acropora palmata*), which in 2006 became one of the first corals to be protected by the U.S. Endangered Species Act.

Coral reefs are in alarming decline worldwide. Fishing techniques that demolish reef structures; runoff and erosion that poison or smother corals; a variety of bacterial and fungal diseases; and rising ocean temperatures due to global climate change threaten the existence of these animals. Becoming adept at propagating corals—both for public display and for reintroduction in the wild—is crucial.

The established way of propagating corals is to take fragments from colonies, glue them to a substrate and let the polyps start multiplying. This imitates the way new colonies arise from

Left: Tiny elkhorn corals grow from planktonic larvae "settled" in Shedd's coral propagation lab. The work is helping to save this endangered species.

storm-shattered corals in the wild. In 1999, Shedd began propagating corals in preparation for Wild Reef, using fragments from other aquariums as well as corals donated by the U.S. Fish and Wildlife Service. (Shedd assists FWS agents to identify illegally imported corals and receives the confiscated animals.)

In 2006, Shedd was part of an international group of aquariums and zoos that teamed up with Project SECORE (SExual COral REproduction). The initiative helps biologists in the field and in the lab to better understand elkhorn reproduction and early life-cycle requirements so that the corals can be raised in-house. In 2008, Shedd aquarists brought back thousands of tiny elkhorn larvae from the annual spawn in Puerto Rico and successfully created the conditions needed for the planktonic creatures to grow by settling on and attaching to specially designed ceramic plates. Shedd is one of three U.S. aquariums and zoos now successfully "settling" elkhorn larvae and providing young corals to more than 20 other aquariums in the United States and Europe. The long-range goal is for the corals to spawn in-house. Shedd is also working with the Curaçao Aquarium to raise and reintroduce elkhorn corals in the Caribbean.

Veterinarians are also studying corals, and Shedd's own "reef medics" are taking the knowledge they're gaining from in-house coral research and applying it to diagnosing and treating coral diseases, both in aquarium settings and in the wild. They are also working on using cultured fragments for reef restoration projects.

Meal Service for 32,000

Imagine preparing breakfast—and often lunch, dinner and snacks, too—for 32,000 customers ordering from 1,500 special menus. That's what an army of Shedd staff members and volunteers do every day. They start with the freshest ingredients . . . but not necessarily with what you'd stock at home.

Several times a week, delivery trucks carrying fresh and frozen seafood and fresh produce pull up at Shedd's loading dock. A portion of this fare is destined for the restaurants and guests' plates, but most of it is for the animals. Each year, Shedd purchases more than 250,000 pounds of restaurant-grade seafood, including 6,000 pounds of mullet, bonita, whole squid and Spanish mackerel for the sharks in Wild Reef, and more than 7,500 pounds of fruits and vegetables, from apples to zucchinis. That includes 720 heads of romaine lettuce for Nickel, the green sea turtle, and edible marigolds, pansies and orchids for the tortoises in Amazon Rising. A local organic farmer extended her CSA program for aquarium employees to include a specially packed bushel of greens, apples and peppers each week for Nickel, iguana Marley and the other vegetarian reptiles.

Shedd also buys 8,000 pounds of prepared gel diets for the fishes each year. These meals are nutritionally balanced for carnivores (loaded with krill and ground-up salmon) and herbivores (heavy on kelp and algae). Insectivores have their own order: 100,000 crickets a year, plus butter worms, wax worms and other wigglers.

In addition to the species-specific diets, the animals receive taxonomically tailored vitamin and mineral supplements: extra vitamin A for the sharks, a formula that includes six B vitamins for the marine mammals and penguins to compensate for any nutrients lost in their frozen fish—and even organic oregano from an area farmers market to provide essential tannin in the diet of the araçari, a small toucan.

A metal triangle calls the sandbar sharks to dinner; a clicker signals the zebra sharks; wooden sticks tapped together draw the mangrove whiptail rays; a wooden dowel run over a notched piece of wood attracts the white-spotted guitarfish; and plastic tongs tapped against the concrete side of the pool means the sawfish's dinner is being served.

These predators have excellent hearing—second only to their famed olfactory sense—but only so-so vision, so the sounds act as dinner bells calling them to their stations if they don't see their shapes. They are seldom, however, late for dinner; usually the arrival of aquarists at the different feeding stations is enough to get the fishes' attention.

Aquarists weigh each piece of food beforehand and measure out the individual meals. Feeding is done by a pair of aquarists, with one giving the animals the food on long tongs while calling out who is eating and how much, and another recording the information and letting the feeder know when each animal has had its allotted portion.

Shedd has three walk-in freezers, two walk-in refrigerators, five kitchens and four additional prep rooms to store and prepare the animals' food.

A Rhythm Band of Dinner Bells

To avoid a genuine feeding frenzy at mealtime, each species of shark and ray in Wild Reef's central habitat has been trained to come to, or "station" at, a specific section of the service deck that rims the top of the 400,000-gallon pool. Aquarists cue each group with its own boldly patterned hand-held shape. The sharks and their relatives also get underwater-audible cues:

*Right: Flowers
are a natural and
nutritious menu
item for Shedd's
tropical reptiles,
including this blue
iguana.*

These records go into an electronic database. By keeping account, aquarists can track any change in a fish's feeding behavior, which can be affected for a variety of reasons, such as the breeding season or by a medical problem. Long-term data for each animal helps the animal care team tell the difference.

Sustainable Seafood

Shedd's Right Bite program is all about choosing sustainable seafood. Whether caught or raised using environmentally friendly methods, the food that the aquarium serves to guests in its restaurants and to the animals in its care is sustainable. Shrimp came off the menu years ago because for every pound caught in large trawl nets, up to 20 pounds of unintentionally entangled sea turtles, large fishes and seabirds—called bycatch—are drowned or fatally injured.

There is, however, one exception: the 12,000 pounds of shrimp consumed by Shedd's sea otters each year. Shedd searched high and low for a company that produces sustainable restaurant-grade shrimp and finally found it in 2006 . . . in Arizona. The company uses water from deep underground to fill its closed-system ponds. After the shrimp is harvested, the water irrigates wheat fields and an olive tree grove before it percolates into the groundwater.

Yet even after the source was located, a larger challenge loomed: Would the sea otters like the shrimp? Their sensitive palates can distinguish between different sources of the same food, and they are known for their dramatic displays of displeasure when given food they don't like. (Picture spitting and vigorous face rubbing.) Fortunately, the otters gobbled it down and asked for more.

Two ponds supply all the shrimp for Shedd's animal collection. By supporting a sustainable source rather than buying shrimp caught from the wild, Shedd prevents as much as 240,000 pounds of marine wildlife from perishing as bycatch each year.

Aquaculture and Eating on the Fly

When they arrive at Shedd, many fishes aren't accustomed to eating food that doesn't wiggle or jiggle. The aquarists start these newcomers on live food that is cultivated in-house to ensure that it is nutritious and free of contaminants. "Clean" food is critical, whether it's used to wean animals onto another diet or feed those that never graduate to prepared food.

The live-foods room is filled with troughs, buckets and tanks of swirling water—each a different color that, on closer look, reveals the nearly microscopic planktonic creatures that so many aquatic animals love to eat. A brown broth is really full of rotifers, which are nutritious for seahorses, moon jellies and corals. A fine-mesh net dipped into a tub of dark water pulls up tiny dots of daphnia, or water fleas, one of the only foods small enough for the mouths of larval freshwater fishes. Tiers of troughs house successive generations of nearly transparent mysis shrimp. It takes five days to raise 2,000 to adult size (about 3/8-inch) for a score of seadragons that suck down 1,200 a day.

All this food has to eat, too. What looks like a large yogurt carton of carrot juice is really a container of brine shrimp eaten by feeder Malaysian river shrimp as well as some of the collection animals. And the only places in the aquarium where algae growth is encouraged are the green-tinged towers where phytoplankton is cultivated for the daphnia and rotifers.

Another area behind the scenes is devoted to raising fruit flies. Cultures are started weekly, and rows of plastic bottles contain the insects at different stages, from maggots to pupae to the adult wingless flies that tiny poison dart frogs find so tasty.

In the 1930s and '40s, when animal nutrition as a science was unknown and resources were scarce, Shedd's "tankmen" fed the fishes horsemeat and smelt—chopped or ground, according to the size of the animal—and daphnia and crayfish collected from ponds in a North Side park.

Handle with Nonconductive Gloves

Electric eels (South American knifefish) can grow to 6 feet long, are coated in slippery slime and breathe air through their mouths. They get their name from the electric organs that cover three-quarters of their bodies, enabling the fish to deliver a 600-volt jolt to anything—or anyone—that threatens them.

When a 4-foot electric eel in Amazon Rising needed a suspicious growth examined and biopsied, Shedd's aquarists, veterinarians and designers summoned all their technical ingenuity to create equipment and a treatment procedure that would be safe for him and his handlers. It was like nothing ever done before at Shedd—or any other aquarium or zoo.

To address the electrocution hazard, Shedd's team members devised a 4-foot-long, 6-inch-diameter clear acrylic tube with drain holes that would allow them to handle the animal without directly touching him. The tube would also hold him in place during the procedure.

Aquarists donned long, thick rubber gloves and used nonconductive nets to move the eel from his habitat to a large rubber tub that was filled with water and an anesthetic drug for fishes. An acoustic device monitored electrical impulses while a voltmeter cabled to a computer monitor displayed peak discharges.

Once the animal was considered safe to handle, showing no signs of movement or electrical discharges, he was transferred to the acrylic tube. The

Opposite: Aquarists wearing nonconductive gloves use an acrylic tube to move an electric eel to a tub of anesthesia-treated water. The fish required a biopsy.

Left: The electric eel's head and body are pitted with electro-receptors to detect prey. Its long, electricity-producing tail begins behind the fins.

veterinary team pumped anesthetic water through his mouth to his gills while he was out of the water. With the animal unconscious, the team made radiographs, weighed him, took biopsy sections and cleaned and sutured the tumor site in less than 20 minutes.

The biopsy revealed a cancerous growth that would have to be removed. Before they could perform surgery, though, the veterinarians needed an MRI to see the extent of the mass. The eel would have to be transported to a veterinary specialty clinic 33 miles from Chicago.

A large amount of water and basic life-support equipment had to be prepared to accompany the animal. During the MRI, the eel would have to be immobile for 40 to 60 minutes, requiring a constant flow of anesthesia into his gills. Because of the strong electromagnetic field in the room, Shedd's medical team would not be able to use its standard anesthesia machine, which is run by mechanical pumps. And wastewater would have to be channeled away from the MRI unit and into a drain.

The team members designed a new 6-foot acrylic tube to address water containment and drainage, adding Velcro straps and a neoprene lining to better secure the eel. Then they designed and built a nonmechanical anesthesia delivery system that worked by gravity and air pressure to supply water to the fish at the desired constant flow rate.

The anesthesia procedure at the clinic was similar to the one at Shedd. The MRI took about 45 minutes. After reviewing the digital images and determining that the eel was stable, the surgeon and veterinarians went ahead and removed the tumor.

Having established the successful protocol, Shedd's veterinarians can now safely give electric eels routine medical exams, short-circuiting serious health problems in these once-untouchable fish. Shedd's animal health team shared what they'd learned in a scientific paper—voted the best paper presentation at a conference of North American zoo veterinary technicians.

Steps to a Career: Mentoring at Shedd

Shedd Aquarium is a magnet for kids who love dolphins, fishes, oceans, reefs, rivers and anything else aquatic. And the attraction is mutual: The aquarium loves to nurture that passion in budding scientists. From its on-site classes and field studies in the Bahamas in the early 1970s, Shedd's offerings for teens have multiplied and are now coordinated in a mentoring ladder. Beginning in middle school, students from the Chicago area can literally get their hands and feet wet with like-minded kids (and with more than one Shedd educator who also went through the mentoring program) in successive curricula that can take them into college.

Programs range from Club Shedd, a monthly forum for teens to discuss conservation issues and explore career opportunities in the aquatic sciences, to Great Lakes ecology, in which the world's largest body of fresh water—right outside Shedd's doors—is turned into a classroom. Other programs include Shedd Stewards,

Students at the Chicago Math and Science Academy implemented a much-wanted paper recycling program at their school with guidance from Shedd's community mentor program. The kids plan to expand to comingled recycling and to compost lunchroom waste as part of their long-term project to "green" their school environment.

involving teens in hands-on fieldwork such as biodiversity surveys and habitat restoration in collaboration with other organizations. Whatever the program, the emphasis is on immersive outdoor experiences.

Certainly the most influential program has been Shedd's award-winning high school marine biology course, which began in 1974. Each year, 20 select high school students from Illinois and surrounding states spend a week at Shedd learning island ecology, community-based marine conservation and field research methods. Then they apply this knowledge during a week of fieldwork in the Bahamas aboard Shedd's research vessel. During this immersive experience, snorkeling students come face to face with their study subjects. High school marine biology has launched scores of careers in marine science, education, animal training and conservation, and graduates of the program can be found working in universities, laboratories and field research sites around the world. One such alum divides his time between studying endangered iguanas

in the Bahamas and managing Shedd Aquarium's field conservation and research programs.

Shedd's mentoring program is building the next generation of aquatic scientists, environmental stewards and informed citizens who have a lifelong interest in science and conservation.

Great Lakes Conservation

Through the years, exhibits in Shedd's Local Waters gallery have reflected and interpreted dramatic changes in the Great Lakes ecosystem, while public programs and activities such as beach cleanups have given area residents opportunities to learn and do more to protect the Great Lake that defines Chicago. As the health of the lakes became a more pressing concern, Shedd took its own responsibility to a higher level and a wider audience with the launch of its Great Lakes public awareness initiative in 2005.

Shedd's strengths in communication, education and community involvement, coupled with its location in the largest metropolitan area in the Great Lakes region, make it a trusted voice for Great Lakes conservation. Focusing on the current issues of habitat loss and degradation, water use and diversion, invasive species, and water quality, Shedd educates people on the urgent threats to the Great Lakes. At the same time, it promotes personal stewardship, offering practical, effective solutions through everyday actions. Shedd is also a venue for forums on Great Lakes issues, allowing stakeholders from government, commerce, conservation and the public to come together to address the problems facing the world's largest freshwater resource.

Shedd's mission, through its animal collection and its programs, is to inspire people to make a difference. The aquarium has a significant impact on the 2 million people who walk through its doors every year, including 350,000 schoolchildren. It interacts with millions more through its community programs and social media, which has brought it an immediate international network of fans. Shedd is about animals, and it's about people—bringing them together at the best, most respected and most amazing aquarium in the world.

in the Bahamas and managing Shedd Aquarium's field conservation and research programs.

Shedd's mentoring program is building the next generation of aquatic scientists, environmental stewards and informed citizens who have a lifelong interest in science and conservation.

Great Lakes Conservation

Through the years, exhibits in Shedd's Local Waters gallery have reflected and interpreted dramatic changes in the Great Lakes ecosystem, while public programs and activities such as beach cleanups have given area residents opportunities to learn and do more to protect the Great Lake that defines Chicago. As the health of the lakes became a more pressing concern, Shedd took its own responsibility to a higher level and a wider audience with the launch of its Great Lakes public awareness initiative in 2005.

Shedd's strengths in communication, education and community involvement, coupled with its location in the largest metropolitan area in the Great Lakes region, make it a trusted voice for Great Lakes conservation. Focusing on the current issues of habitat loss and degradation, water use and diversion, invasive species, and water quality, Shedd educates people on the urgent threats to the Great Lakes. At the same time, it promotes personal stewardship, offering practical, effective solutions through everyday actions. Shedd is also a venue for forums on Great Lakes issues, allowing stakeholders from government, commerce, conservation and the public to come together to address the problems facing the world's largest freshwater resource.

Shedd's mission, through its animal collection and its programs, is to inspire people to make a difference. The aquarium has a significant impact on the 2 million people who walk through its doors every year, including 350,000 schoolchildren. It interacts with millions more through its community programs and social media, which has brought it an immediate international network of fans. Shedd is about animals, and it's about people—bringing them together at the best, most respected and most amazing aquarium in the world.

Shedd
AQUARIUM

The John G. Shedd Aquarium, a not-for-profit organization dedicated to public education and conservation, is one of the world's largest indoor aquariums. It houses more than 32,000 aquatic animals, representing 1,500 species of fishes, reptiles, amphibians, invertebrates, birds, and marine and freshwater mammals from waters around the world. Since its opening in 1930, the aquarium's mission has been to enhance public understanding of aquatic life and connect guests to the natural world, inspiring them to protect and preserve the planet.

PHOTO CREDITS

Unless otherwise stated, all photos are copyright
John G. Shedd Aquarium.
Shedd photography by Brenna Hernandez and:
Ilze Berzins
Charon Brock
Patrice Ceisel
Walter H. Chute
Karen Furnweger
Jan Kanter
Edward G. Lines Jr.
Jonathan Mathias
Colby Mitchell
Heidi Zeiger
and the Shedd Aquarium photo archives

Additional photography:
Chicago History Museum DN-0066830: 17
Courtesy Curt Teich Postcard/Lake County
   Discovery Museum: 27
Jupiterimages/Photos.com: Jacket, 5, 9, 23, 41, 55
Library of Congress: 14, 15, 18, 28, 29
Copyright Doug Snower: 47
Courtesy of Target Corporation: 16, 19

BECKON BOOKS

This edition is published by Beckon Books in cooperation with Event Network. Beckon Books is an imprint of FRP Books, 2451 Atrium Way, Nashville, Tennessee 37214. Beckon publishes custom books for cultural attractions, corporations, and non-profit organizations.

President: Christopher G. Capen
Design/Production: Monika Stout
Editor: Betsy Holt
www.beckonbooks.com
877-311-0155

Event Network is the retail partner of the John G. Shedd Aquarium and is proud to benefit and support Shedd's mission to connect people to the living world.
www.eventnetwork.com

FRP, Inc. is a wholly owned subsidiary of Southwestern/Great American, Inc.
Nashville, Tennessee

ISBN 978-1-935442-03-5
Printed in Canada
10 9 8 7 6 5 4 3 2 1